Kuneku

Kunekune pigs as pets

Kunekune pigs book for keeping, pros and cons, care, housing, diet and health.

by

Roger Rodendale

Table of Contents

Introduction

Do you fancy having a pig as a pet? Or are you a small farm owner who wants to have a passel of pigs of your own? Either way, Kunekune pigs are ideal for you. These pigs are known to make wonderful pets, as they are extremely intelligent and fun to be around.

These pigs are not as popular as the pot-bellied pig because they are not as easily available. However, when you find the right source, you will soon find yourself biased to this breed of pigs simply because they are extremely loving and capable of learning several tricks as well.

These pigs are known to be more trusting in nature towards human beings, which also makes them perfect for families. They look extremely cute with their unique hair that comes in a myriad of colors and patterns. Whether it is a tri colored Kunekune or a spotted one, you will surely fall in love with these pigs when you see them.

The personality of the Kunekune is responsible for the growing interest in these animals as pets. Kunekune pigs are more likely to come when called and are also affectionate towards their family in comparison to other breeds of pigs.

These smaller sized pigs are ideal for different environments. They are gentle beings that are also used in several therapy programs and also in pet shows.

When you bring a Kunekune pig home, you must understand the breed thoroughly in order to be able to provide the necessary care. These animals have very specific dietary requirements and also have some healthcare necessities that you need to provide in order to pursue your pet to its fullest potential.

If you are a beginner in the world of pigs, then you are in for a series of surprises. Although pigs are usually associated with laziness, you will realize that your pet is anything but that. They not only need a good amount of exercise and physical activity but also need ample mental stimulation in order to be healthy and happy.

This book is prefect for you if you want to learn more about the Kunekune pig before bringing one home as a pet. It covers various subjects such as the origin, natural history, dietary requirements, breeding, healthcare requirements and more to help you understand your responsibilities as a Kunekune owner.

The contents of this book are based on detailed research carried out with other Kunekune owners. That way all the tips and the information that you get is authentic and extremely practical.

Above all, the goal of this book is to make sure that you are ready to become a parent to a Kunekune pig. They are just as demanding as any other pet. You need to ensure that you give them ample attention, care and love in order for them to thrive and stay in the pink of their health.

Once you are sure that you can afford and manage one of these fantastic animals, you are in for the ride of a lifetime!

Chapter 1: Introduction to the Kunekune Pig

With the growing popularity of the Kunekune pigs as pets, a lot has been studied and researched about the breed. Although they are native to New Zealand, these pigs have become a global favorite among farm owners and pig lovers.

This chapter tells you everything that you need to know about the history, origin and traits of the Kunekune pigs.

1. Physical Traits

The Kunekune pig is one of the smallest of all domesticated pigs. The name Kunekune comes from a Maori word which means 'fat and round'. This is perfectly descriptive of the appearance of this unusual variety of pigs.

They are among the smaller breeds that are found in New Zealand. However, these pigs are also considered to be relatively large because they tend to be overweight.

At first glance, this pig has a rounded body with short legs and a short snout. The face of the pig, which is quite small, along with the stubby nose gives the pig the look of a Disney character.

The hair on the body is one of the most characteristic traits of the Kunekune pig. These pigs have pire pire or strands of hair that appear like tassels on the lower jaw. These tassels, also known as wattles, may grow up to 4cms in length. The tassels are not found in all Kunekune pigs, however. Sometimes the pig may even have just one tassel. The tassel could also fall off sometimes because it is not attached properly or because of any injuries in the past.

When breeding, only the pigs that have these tassels are chosen. Sometimes the pigs without tassels may be bred. There could also be a cross between a tasseled pig and a non-tasseled one, resulting in offspring without any characteristic tassels. This physical trait helps you distinguish between the purebred Kunekune and the mixed varieties.

The color of the coat can vary significantly. Commonly, the coat color is black, brown, black and white, tan, gold or cream. They may also have patches or spots of different colors on the body. The texture of the coat may also vary. Some pigs have silky and smooth hair; others may have curly hair that looks ruffled and unkempt. The texture of the coat can also change as per the season. At times, you will observe a very wide difference in the summer coat and the winter coat. These pigs also tend to lose a lot of hair in the warmer months.

These pigs usually grow up to 70cms in height and may weigh close to 100 kilos.

Official breed standards
Commercially bred Kunekune pigs look quite different to the ones that are bred specifically for show purposes. The latter have to adhere to the standards set by the various Kunekune pig societies across the globe. These standards earn points and determine the placement of your pig in a particular show. One of the most important traits of show Kunekune pigs is the head. The head shows if the pig is just a grazer and does not root. This characteristic is unique to Kunekune pigs and will fetch several points when the animal is being judged in a show.

If you are interested in entering your pig into shows, then these standards are necessary for you to know.

General appearance of the pig

- **Form of the body:** The body should be deep, level and long. Sows should be about 250 pounds in weight while boars weigh 300 pounds. The weight should be the result of fat and firm flesh.

- **Quality of the body:** The bone structure should vary from medium to heavy. The flesh and fat should be even. The skin should be clean and the hair should cover the body uniformly.

- **Condition of the body:** The pig should appear well balanced. The covering of flesh should be deep and uniform. In areas that provide contours to the body, especially, the fat should be uniformly deposited.

Typical characteristics

- **Head of the pig:** The face should be broad and dished. The snout must be upturned and short. The teeth should be visible showing that the pig is a grazer and does not root.

- **Ears:** The ears can range from semi-lopped to pricked. They should be inclined forwards, however.

- **Wattles:** A minimum of two wattles must be present and they should be well attached.

- **Neck:** The length of neck can vary from short to medium.

- **Body:** The shoulders should be leveled and should be proportionate with the rump. The front legs should be placed at a moderate distance from one another so that the chest looks wide. The hams must be well formed.

- **Back:** The back must appear strong, with a small arch that looks proportionate.

- **Tail:** The curled and crooked tail is trademark of Kunekune pigs. Straight tails are undesirable for competitions.

- **Legs:** The length of the legs varies from medium to short. They need to appear strong with upright pasterns.

- **Feet:** The feet should be medium sized, even and closed.

- **Skin and hair:** The coat can have any pattern except for the belted variety. All textures are accepted in competitions. However, belted Kunekunes are disqualified from competition.

- **Temperament:** The pigs should have a placid nature.

- **Sexual characteristics:** There are specific traits that are desirable for the males and the females respectively.

Male Kunekune pigs:

- The head should be coarse.
- The neck must have a slight arch but must appear full.
- The forequarters should be larger and heavier in comparison to the hindquarters. Older pigs should have shields that make this difference more visible.
- The frame must be strong but preferably smooth.
- The body should be low, deep and long.
- The legs should be strong and between medium and short in height. Pasterns should be straight.

Female Kunekune pigs

- There must be no signs of coarseness on the body.
- The frame should be feminine. The contours are sharp and neat in the females.
- The width of the body from the front and from the back should be the similar and uniform.
- The body must have an abundant length that allows her to grow litter and farrow easily.
- The teats should be spaced evenly and none of them should be blind.

2. History of Kunekune Pigs

Very little is known about the origin of the Kunekune pig. As a result, there have been several theories about this. How Kunekune pigs came to New Zealand is still a highly debated subject. These pigs, according to an article published in the year 1945 in the Journal of Agriculture, states that these pigs may have originated from the Old Poland breed found in China. The author, J W Pierson states that these Polish pigs have a similar black and white pattern. In addition, they are the only ones in the world besides the Kunekune to have the tassels on their skin. The question that remains is: how did these pigs get to New Zealand?

Kunekune Origin Theories

The origin theories about the Kunekune pigs in New Zealand are as follows:

1. **They were brought in by the Maoris in canoes**
   The modern day Kunekune pigs seem to have some geographical link with the areas that have very strong Maori history and attachments. This includes Northland, East Coast, Waikato and Bay of Plenty. This also confirms the fact that these pigs have been

associated with the Maoris for a long time. There are chances that these pigs were part of the Maori settlements as early as the time of immigrants from Polynesia.

According to this theory, the Kunekune pigs were brought to New Zealand when the Maoris made their way there in canoes. This theory has been quite disapproved due to fossil evidence. No signs of these pigs were found in New Zealand until the later part of the 1700s. This is when New Zealand was discovered by the Europeans, who often let their pigs loose on the offshore islands. They were then let loose even on the mainland.

Another theory states that even though the pigs were brought in by the Maori in canoes, most of them were unable to survive the trip. It was common for the Polynesians to breed pigs for food, so it is most likely that this breed of pigs originated in Asia or in Indonesia. They were then transported to New Zealand by the Polynesian travelers.

Evidences of pig breeds quite similar to the Kunekune were found by Sir Peter Buck. These fossils were similar to the ones that were found in Tahiti around 950AD. This is where the Maoris originally came from.

The pigs that were found in Tahiti were also named the Kunekune. Therefore it is quite possible that when the Maoris made their way to New Zealand, they brought these pigs back with them. However, since the journey was long and difficult, most of these pigs did not survive.

If the Maoris had succeeded in bringing these pigs to New Zealand safely, they may have thrived quite well. It is now believed that these pigs were actually introduced into New Zealand in the year 1796 by Captain Cook.

He has made records of Maori takes that speak of a land to the north west of New Zealand where the people commonly ate 'pauka'. This is the Samoan word for pig. However, it is believed that the word comes from the English word 'porker', making it somewhat insignificant.

2. Relation to the Captain Cooker Pigs

According to this theory, these pigs are genetically similar to the feral pigs in New Zealand called the Captain Cooker. It is believed that these pigs were brought to New Zealand by Captain Cook during his voyage to New Zealand in the year 1796. These pigs were meant to provide food for him and his crew. These pigs were then bred with some domestic pigs that were aboard his ship to produce the modern day Kunekune.

This theory is not quite credible because of the presence of tassels on the chin of the Kunekune pigs. In order to account for the presence of the tassels it would be necessary that the pigs aboard the ship were either Wessex, Middle White, Tamworth or Berkshire pigs that descended from the Old Poland Chinese pigs. However, there is a good chance that these pigs were brought to New Zealand by Captain Cook as a source of food. So, even though this theory is not very popular among biologist, it is not entirely impossible.

There is another version which states that breeding between the Old Poland Pig and the Captain Cooker may have led to the modern day Kunekune. This breeding may have taken place after Captain Cook introduced the Cookers into New Zealand. Around the same time, Old Poland pigs had gained a lot of popularity in the United States. It is possible that some of these pigs were brought into the island by the whalers from America. They were then distributed in the mainland by the gold miners.

3. Releases by De Surville and Captain Cook

While it is widely presumed that these pigs were introduced in the year 1793 by Captain Cook, the theory is still debated. It was believed that Captain Cook exchanged the pigs that he had on board for fresh meat from the Maoris. However, the pigs that were introduced did not breed well and therefore, failed to survive.

Some of the first recorded Kunekune pigs in New Zealand are believed to have been brought by a French explorer named De Surville. Records show that a sow and a boar were given to the Maori tribe in the year 1769 in Doubtless Bay. However, these pigs, it is believed, were killed and used as food before they could breed.

One board and two sows were also released by Captain Furneax during the second voyage of Captain Cook to New Zealand in the year 1773. However, even these were consumed as food by the Maoris.

During the latter part of the same year, two pairs of pigs were given to the Maori tribes living in Cape Kidnappers. Another sow was given to the Maoris in Queen Charlotte. Three sows and a boar were also released in West Bay.

A year after this, one pair was released in Cannibal Cove. And, in the last visit in the year 1773, Captain Cook gave the Maoris another pair.

4. Gifts from the king

This is one of the most well documented theories, as it corresponds to the kidnapping of two important Maori people.

The Norfolk Islanders captured two Maoris at the Cavalli Islands in order to teach them how to weave flax and dress themselves. One of the kidnapped Maori was the Chieftain and the other one was a priest. They did not have any experience with these tasks as they were reserved for the women and men from the lower rung of the tribe.

The kidnapped Maoris were then returned to New Zealand in the year 1793. As a token of apology, Lieutenant Governor Philip Gidley King sent back two boars and ten sows from the Norfolk Island. These pigs then bred in New Zealand following which the Lieutenant sent four boards and six sows more to the Maoris.

The culture of exchanging gifts with their neighbors and their family members resulted in the increase in population of these pigs across the island.

5. Sealers and Whalers

An unpublished paper by GF Angus talks about the genetics, origins and the release of the Kunekune and Captain Cooker pigs into New Zealand. According to this paper, these pigs were originally introduced by explorers from Spain. They were then domesticated by the sealers and whalers from Europe.

From the year 1790, several European and American explorers, whalers and sealers made their way to New Zealand. They attempted to created colonies of pigs for breeding on the off shore island around New Zealand. These pigs would be the source of food in case of a shipwreck and would also feed the castaways.

These pigs were then offered for trade to the Maoris. The pigs were exchanged for muskets and tobacco by the American Whalers who visited Russell. Pigs were held in high value by the Maoris. Therefore, they were responsible for the breed spreading across the island as they were offered as gifts and tokens. Some of these pigs escaped and gave rise to feral populations.

As the number of Europeans in New Zealand increased, the numbers of these pigs began to diminish. These pigs were a source of food for the Maoris but were used up by the Europeans. These pigs became endangered with only a few numbers in Waharoa district and Te Kuiti.

Later, John Simister and Micheal Willis, two wildlife park owners, began to work on the populations of these pigs in New Zealand. With just about 50 purebred varieties left, they had to look for pigs that could be bred everywhere in the country. They then bout 4 boars and 10 sows from various small farm owners across New Zealand.

These pigs were then brought to South Island for breeding. Attempts to keep the populations high in the North were also being made at the same time. Several pigs were kept at the Hilldale Game Farm located in Hamilton. These pigs were then spread across New Zealand and also across the globe to prevent any extinction of the species altogether.

Kunekune Pigs in England
These pigs were brought to the UK in the year 1992 by Andrew Calveley and Zoe Lindop, who worked for several years in New Zealand. They were charmed by this unique breed ad then met Michael Willis to learn more about them. They realized that this breed was quite endangered and therefore decided that they should import a few of them to Britain. These pigs were only found in New Zealand and it was necessary that another country also have a small population. In case a disease broke out in their native land, the species would be wiped out if not bred in another country.

A wide range of these pigs were then bred specifically for them by Michael Willis. He believed that they need to have a varied genetic stock to take back to Britain. In case they brought just one variety back, it would not represent the breed entirely and would not be useful for increasing the numbers.

Later, in the year 1993, two more blood lines were imported to the UK by Zoe. Three years later, Andy Case imported three bloodlines more into the UK. Today, the population is well established in all of Britain.

The British Kunekune Society was set up in the year 1993. Since the originally imported pigs were complete pedigrees, it became necessary to create a study book to record their history and create guidelines for registering the pigs in Britain. This society was started with this objective and also works for the welfare of this breed. Currently, the society has 500 members. Each year four newsletters are produced by the society which is suitable for anyone who is interested in this breed.

Kunekune Pigs in the USA
These pigs were first brought into the USA in the year 1995 by Katie Rigby. She started her own breeding program with pigs that were brought in from New Zealand. This breeding program was a closed one. As a result, only neutered and spayed pigs were sold as pets. Today, not many pigs from this bloodline are seen in the USA.

In the year 2005, another lot of these pigs were imported to the USA. This time, the pigs were brought in from the UK. These pigs were imported specifically to set up breeding programs of these pigs in the USA. This import led to a wider genetic stock and also led to a more successful breeding program.

There were two more imports in the year 2010 and 2012. Today, the American Kunekune Society sets all the breed standards, guidelines for registering the pigs and also for showing and exhibiting Kunekune pigs in the USA.

3. Natural habitat
Kunekune pigs thrive in pastures and in woodlands. These pigs do best when kept outdoors, so if you are bringing a Kunekune pig home, one of the biggest considerations is space. You must have a pen that is at least 2m in size for a single pig. We will discuss in greater detail about housing your Kunekune pig.

4. Coat coloration of Kunekune Pigs
The cells of all pigs contain DNA which is then paired into 38 chromosomes. Genes are the result of the sequence of these DNA strands present in the chromosomes. In pigs, 20000 such genes have been identified.

Genes have one particular function each. Although they do interact with one another, it is these genes that result in the different physical characteristics of an animal. Learning about the color genetics of Kunekune pigs is extremely important if you are planning to breed your pig.

So, let us first understand how color genetics works. The color of the offspring is dependent on the genes carried by the parents and the interaction between these genes. For instance, in the case of a black Kunekune piglet, the dominant gene is black. This means that either of the parents carried a black gene that is expressed in the offspring.

All pigs have 2 gene sets. One of them is the one that you see, or the dominant gene, and the other one is hidden or recessive. Sometimes, you can also have a double dominant gene, which means that both are dominant. In other cases, one is dominant and one is recessive.

There are some complex combinations that are also possible due to interactions with a separate gene. For instance, even with parents having the black gene, you may have a brown offspring because of a separate gene called the Chinchilla gene.

When pigs are bred, one of the genes can be passed on to the offspring. So, you may have unexpected results when it comes to the color of the offspring. As breeders continue to produce a certain type of coloration in their pigs, one of the colors will become more frequent. This is normally seen when they choose to have a color which is the result of a recessive gene such as ginger. If you breed enough ginger pigs, chances are that certain dominant genes are lost from the pigs that you breed.

Color genes in Kunekune pigs

When it comes to Kunekune pigs, there are 5 primary gene locations. These are:

- Extenstion (E)
- Agouti (A)
- Chinchilla (Ch)
- Dilute
- White Spotting Genes

You can have more than one type for each of these gene locations. This means that they are not restricted to just 2 genes in each location. For instance, the extension gene location has 4 choices of genes. These gene locations can also influence each other, resulting in different patterns and colors. The final outcome that you see is the result of these 5 gene locations working together with each other.

The basic color of the body is influenced by the Extension genes. This gives you four possibilities including:

- Ed which is dominant black.
- E which is normal black.
- ej which is dark ginger with either black patches or black spots
- e which is just dark ginger.

If the E gene location occurs in a pig, you are able to see the Agouti gene. If the pig is not E type, then this gene is blocked, preventing you from seeing the agouti colors. There are three types of agouti genes, namely As, Ay and Aw. If the pigs have the E gene location along with the Agouti gene location, they tend to be black, brown or the true agouti color, which has yellow tips on the body hair and a light underbelly.

In the Agouti type, the piglets tend to have stripes on the coat that are longitudinal. This is almost like the camouflage that is seen in young ones of many species in the wild.

The Chinchilla gene is the third type of gene that is found in Kunekune pigs. This trait is also seen in other varieties of pigs like the Berkshire pigs. The main color of the coat may be modified if the Chinchilla gene is dominant in the pig. Even the black coat can be modified to leave black patches on a predominantly cream body. Even the ginger variety is normally changed to a cream color.

There is another gene that behaves like a Dilute gene. This makes a particular color look duller than normal. It can vary the intensity of different coat colors. This gene is responsible for some ginger pigs looking darker and the other ginger pigs looking paler.

The last gene location is the White Spotting Gene. This is a recessive gene. It results in the appearance of certain patches and spots that are white in color all over the body. This is also associated with a kind of modifying gene that is responsible for the type and size of the white marking on the pig's body.

What you need to understand is that black is certainly the most dominant color when it comes to Kunekine pigs. Following that is the agouti gene. Ginger pigs with black spots are the next level. In some cases the ginger color can also be modified into cream and the black spots may be modified to brown by the Chinchilla genes. The most recessive variety in coat coloration is the plain ginger. This can also be modified to cream by the Chinchilla genes.

The white color that is seen in Kunekune pigs is quite different from the white coloration that is seen in other varieties of white colored pigs. There are usually ginger tones on a predominantly cream colored body. They also tend to have greyish skin that can have some serious sunburn. It is possible that you will get an offspring that is white in color if you cross any Kunekune pig with a white colored pig. The reason for this is that with other species, the dominant gene is white.

Chapter 2: The Kunekune as a Pet

There is no doubt that Kunekune pigs make the most wonderful pets. These animals are adorable to look at, are easier to manage in comparison to other miniature pigs and also have a great personality.

This chapter tells you what you can expect when you take the responsibility of a pet pig. Not many people know enough about raising pigs. This means that you will have less support when it comes to understanding the requirements of this animal. It is best that you do enough homework about the breed that you bring home so that you are not in for any rude surprises once you have committed to bringing the animal home.

1. What makes Kunekune pigs great pets?

Anyone who has had a Kunekune pig as a pet can vouch for the fact that they make fantastic pets. As long as they have enough room to move around and good food and healthcare, these are among the easiest pets to maintain.

Some Kunekune owners even claim that Kunekunes are the new dogs with their rising popularity as pets. But unlike the dog, you do not have to worry about walking the pig, or fleas and ticks. Of course, there are more reasons than this one for the immense popularity of this breed.

People often believe that pot-bellied pigs are easier to have as pets because of their miniature status. However, after talking to people who have had both breeds of pets, the common consensus is that the Kunekune pig is the right way to go if you are new to the world of pigs and do not have any experience with them.

So what makes the Kunekune pigs a better option as pets in comparison to other pig breeds?

- **They are not skittish around people:** With most pig breeds, the common behavior is to run away when you approach them. Instead, Kunekune pigs are curious creatures and simply love the attention. They will stay near you and will also show keen interest in the activities that you are going about in your day.

  This also means that you do not have to struggle to round them up into their pen at nightfall. They are also easy to catch for examination by the veterinarian or to treat any injuries. With other breeds of pigs, you can expect them to be quite wary of humans. Most of them will only come to you if you have some food to offer to them. If not, they have to really be cornered when you want to catch them or even touch them.

- **They are furry little creatures:** One thing that you will not find with most pig breeds is the hair. This makes it great fun to pet these pigs as well. These hairy pigs, as discussed before, come in several colors and have beautiful patterns on their fur. The wattles are characteristic of this breed, which simply adds to their beauty. If you are looking for a furry and cute pet on your farm, then the Kunekune pig will never disappoint you.

- **They are easier to maintain:** With breeds like the pot-bellied pigs, one of the biggest issues is that they tend to root up your farm or yard to make a big mess. This is one of the reasons why Kunekune pigs are preferred by most farm owners. They are actually beneficial in preserving your pastures instead of simply tearing them down.

- **They are very easy to train:** There are several negative connotations when it comes to pigs. People believe that they are lazy and dull. However, these animals are anything but that. They are highly intelligent beings that respond very well to training. You can even train your Kunekune pigs to perform tricks and solve puzzles. We will talk in detail about the intelligence of these pigs and training tips to help you bond with them.

- **Hassle free daily maintenance:** Although Kunekune pigs are hairy, they do not shed any fur. The fur on their skin is hypoallergenic, so if one of the reasons for not having a pet at home is allergies, then the Kunekune pig is the ideal choice for you. They are generally quite hardy as well. This means that they do not require too many vet visits as long as you provide the right living conditions.

2. The downside of having a Kunekune pig

While Kunekune pigs are delightful to have as pets, there are some issues that may crop up as you raise them. Here are some downsides of choosing a Kunekune pig as a pet:

- **They live really long:** On average, a Kunekune pig can live up to 20 years in captivity. For a pet owner this means that you need to take the responsibility of the pig for so many years. You need to be prepared for the recurring costs for this period. In addition, have you planned your life that far ahead? What if you have a professional commitment that requires you to move out of your current home? What if your pig falls really sick? Unless you are sure that you can handle all this and more, it is not a good idea to jump into the commitment of owning a pig.

- **They tend to develop behavioral issues:** One thing that you need to know about any intelligent being is that they require enough mental stimulation. Without that, they tend to develop several behavioral issues. Although these issues can be corrected with training, it can become quite dangerous if you have children or other pets on your property.

- **They get stressed during extreme weather conditions:** Kunekune pigs are very sensitive to heat. Their general body structure makes harsh summers quite unbearable for them. This leads to several health issues and extreme stress. Without proper care, your pig may develop serious health issues that are expensive to manage. Sometimes you may just have to struggle to keep your pet alive if he does not have proper care during the warmer months. The best way to reduce heat and weather related stress is to keep the Kunekune pig active for the most part. This means that you will have to spend ample time with your pig as well.

3. The highly intelligent Kunekune

One thing that you can be certain about the Kunekune pig is that it is a very intelligent creature. There are several studies and reports that prove, each time, that Kunekune pigs make great pets because of their cognitive skills. This also makes them very entertaining to have at home as pets.

In general, pigs are highly competent socially and can learn new skills easily. There is one skill with pigs that have not been fully explored to date - the ability to learn thorough observation. This is a combination of their social behavior and intelligence, which are both highly revered.

Recent studies on Kunekune pigs revealed that they have the ability to learn from each other. This is a demonstration of learning abilities that are highly developed.

The study was conducted by the Messerli Research Institute of Vetmeduni Vienna. These studies show that piglets can learn a lot of skills by simply observing their mother or any other female in the group. The advantage with pigs is that they also have long-term memory that helps them retain a skill once they have learnt the technique.

This study was recently published in the well-known *Animal Behavior* journal.

Pigs are widely discredited for being dull creatures. In fact, a lot of studies in the past have rendered them quite capable of making any decisions or learning. There have been a few studies that associate this ability with their social behavior. These studies, although published, have not showed any clear results.

Most of these studies are restricted to activities like finding food in new places. While this shows some cognitive skills, it does not demonstrate that they have any highly developed ability to learn.

The real demonstration of any cognitive skills is when the pig is able to copy complex behavior or understand the intention or objective of a certain activity.

This was demonstrated in the study published by the Messerli Research Institute. These studies were conducted on pigs that were free ranging. They observed the Kunekune breed to understand their behavior. The results showed the following:

- **These pigs were capable of learning from their elders**

  The primary objective of this study was to see if there was any vertical transformation of information among pigs. In simple terms, the researchers wanted to understand if any knowledge can be passed from the older generation to the newer one.

  As opposed to most studies that were based on piglets and their interactions with peers, this study was performed on piglets and their ability to learn from their own mother or through another female. It included manipulative tasks that showcased more complex behavior.

  The task in this study involved finding food after sliding the door of a box that contained it. The door opened to the left or the right or in the center. The pigs could use their snout to open these boxes.

  Three groups of six piglets were created. A separate observation compartment was used for two of these groups. This allowed the piglets to observe their mother or another female in order to learn the technique to open the food box. The third group was required to learn how to open the box without observing the mother or an adult female. The objective of having control group was to see if the piglets were predisposed to certain movements of the door which allowed them to open it.

Results of the studies
The control group of piglets showed that they tried every possible technique to open the box. This only confirmed that they did not have any idea or a predisposed skill to open the box. The piglets kept in the observation compartments, however, showed that they had the ability to learn through observation.

This showed that they were capable of reenacting the way the object was moved. Now, one interesting thing is that they displayed the skills that they had learnt mostly on the day after the observation. This means that they took some time to memorize the movement that they had observed and then demonstrated the skill when needed.

In the world of research, the animals that have often been ignored and neglected are pigs. Since the general public does not hold them in very high regard, not much importance has been given to the cognitive skills of the animal.

Kunekune pigs also have great long term memory
The non-observer piglets also showed some great performance during these studies. It was noticed that the animals that had figured out the solution to the food box were actually able to remember it. This was seen in piglets who figured it out with fewer attempts.

When studied half a year later, these piglets were still able to remember the solution to the food box. This showed that the animals, without a doubt, had great long-term memory.

According to this study, the way the pigs are kept and maintained plays a very important role in their ability to learn socially. It was found that free range piglets that lived in large groups had better skills. This triggered the social intelligence of the animals. It is a good idea to keep this in mind whenever you are making any changes in the living conditions of your pigs.

For instance, if you have plans to change the housing of the pigs, remember that the older members of the group can have a big influence on the younger ones. That way you can house them in a manner that allows more interaction and triggers better learning in the little ones. This can also lead to the transfer of several desirable behavior traits.

4. Natural behavior of pigs

Before you bring home a Kunekune pig, understanding their natural behavior is extremely important. This will help you figure out why your pig is behaving in a certain way and will also teach you how to handle certain types of behavior.

The most important thing to know is how pigs interact in groups. This behavior can be used to create your own social hierarchy in your home and ensure that you have a pig that is well behaved and is able to fit into your home from the first day.

Social behavior in pigs

Pig display social behavior that is highly developed. Within just hours of being born, piglets understand dominant relationships among their littermates. Over time, they form a hierarchy that is stable.

This is one of the reasons why you will see pigs from the same litter fight very rarely. Fights in groups of pigs normally occur when you bring two mature males of the same social hierarchy together. This is normally seen during the breeding period.

You may find that your Kunekune pigs are fighting a lot during the autumn months. This is when food is also reserved to patches. However, pigs are quick to establish which one is higher ranking and which one is lower ranking and the submissive behavior of the latter resolves these issues.

The early associations that are formed between piglets are carried well into their adulthood. This is seen more often with the females. Studies show that pigs have the ability to remember about 30 associations that they have formed with individuals over their lifetime. This is the reason why groups of pigs are often restricted to 20 individuals.

The social units of pigs are basically formed by one or more females and their piglets. The other individuals are often loosely associated with the group. The male pigs only join the females and their groups during the rutting season which begins in October. For the most part, male pigs remain solitary. There may be groups of only makes that are formed sometimes in the latter months of the summer season.

Commonly, piglets are born in spring. However, sows can have piglets all through the year. If they have the right feeding and breeding conditions, a sow can give birth two times in a year. In a group all the females tend to have piglets around the same time.

Maternal behavior in pigs

When they are born, piglets tend to be very active. In fact, they get on their feet in just a few minutes of being born. Each piglet will sample the individual teat of the mother before attaching itself to one. This is the teat that the piglet will suckle on for the entire nursing period. This is a very important behavior trait that allows the piglets to recognize their littermates in the future based on the hierarchy.

Every piglet that is born is different in size. The ones that are smallest are born last. The piglets that are bigger in size attach themselves to the anterior teats as they produce more milk. They tend to be very defensive about the teat that they attach themselves to.

This also shows that piglets that are the strongest are provided with the most amount of food. This increases their chances of survival, although it could mean that the weaker ones do not make it. If the food available to the sow is scarce, only the stronger piglets will survive. However, if they have enough food, all the piglets may thrive.

Piglets suckle every alternate hour and sleep in the time in between. When it is feeding time, the sow will normally lie on her side and grunt to her little ones, calling upon them to feed.

Once they learn this behavior, the piglets come to the sow on their own. To keep themselves warm, piglets will also huddle together near the udder of the mother. This is the time when the sow is inactive for the most part.

Activity patterns in pigs

It has been observed that pigs have two activity peaks in a day. They are most active early in the morning and in the evening. After dusk, they prefer to rest. In the wild, it has been observed that boars may develop nocturnal activity just to avoid being disturbed by people.

When they are in a social group, the resting and feeding time is synchronized. During the colder months, pigs tend to construct warm nests for themselves.

Pigs like to maintain their skin in good condition. For this, they will either rub their bodies against trees or will roll in wallows. This is also useful in removing any parasites from the bodies of the pigs.

Wallowing is very important for pigs, as it allows them to cool their bodies down. Pigs do not have any sweat glands. They only have a few on their snout. Therefore, they need to cool off by wallowing, sometimes in their own urine and dung.

When they are in a social group, it is important for pigs to stay in close proximity of each other. They will normally be seen lying together when they are resting. This is also useful in preventing any loss of heat from the body.

When they are at the peak of their activity level, pigs are often seen searching for food.

Feeding habits of pigs
Pigs are known to be opportunists when it comes to food. They are omnivores and will eat just about anything. Pigs love to eat a variety of foods but prefer a diet that is predominantly made of fiber. They like to look for their food and then eat it. Foraging is a common habit in pigs. They love to sniff around and pick their food. Then they ensure that it is well chewed before it is swallowed.

In the months of summer and spring, Kunekune pigs are often seen feeding on tubers, grass and small invertebrates. In autumn, they like to eat nuts, berries and acorns. This is in preparation for winters when food is usually scarce.

In the wild, some varieties of pigs are also known to eat vertebrates such as turtles and snakes. They also consume eggs of birds that form nests on the ground. They may even prey on certain rodents.

Urinating and defecating
It is very important for pigs to have a specific area to defecate and urinate. They normally choose the natural corridors in between trees and bushes. When they are raised on a farm, pigs prefer to defecate and urinate in areas that are away from the resting area. If you see a pig urinating and defecating the area reserved for resting, chances are that he is suffering from heat stress.

5. Considerations before bringing a pig home
If you are leaning towards the idea of bringing a Kunekune pig home, then here are some considerations that you need to make before making that final commitment. People know very little about keeping pigs and often believe that they are yard animals who just need food and water and can be left alone. However, they are very social creatures and can be quite demanding at times, making it necessary for you to ask yourself these questions before you actually go out and find the perfect one for yourself:

Do you have time for your pig?
As discussed before, Kunekune pigs have a very highly developed social structure. These animals require ample social interaction and should be

kept active if you plan to bring one home as a pet. If you have a busy schedule that does not allow you to interact with your pet pig, you must be prepared for a lot of destructive behavior. This includes squealing for your attention, tearing paper, knocking down trash cans, ruining your clothes and a lot more.

Destructive behavior in pigs is the result of a lack of proper mental stimulation. While they can be trained to behave well, this can be overwhelming for a new owner. They also develop issues such as aggressive behavior when they are not given enough attention. They may charge at you with loud grunts.

If you feel like you cannot invest enough time in a pig, you may choose to have a pair or a group of pigs. This also means that the costs will increase. They also need more space in order to thrive.

Another important consideration is if your job requires you to travel frequently. This means that you will have to make arrangements when you are gone. Not all pet sitters have enough experience with pigs, making it harder for you to find someone who can take good care of your pet. Before you bring the pig home, make sure that you have chosen various options to ensure your pig proper care while you are away.

Can you afford to bring one home?
Kunekune pigs, as discussed before, will be around for at least 20 years or so. This means that you have to sustain them and make sure that you have the financial ability to provide for them for this period of time.

There are several costs associated with raising Kunekune pigs. Here is a list of expenses that you should keep in mind and prepare yourself for:

- **Cost of the pig:** Kunekune pigs are priced between $300-500 or £100-150 depending on the type of pig that you buy. Normally, if you buy a pig that is neutered or spayed, it will cost you much less. The cost may increase if the pig has already been potty trained and socialized by the breeder.

- **Housing:** You need to have a shelter built for your pigs to keep them safe from any heat related stress. This will cost you at least $300 or £150 for the material alone. If you have someone else constructing it for you, you will have to add labor costs as well. This is a one-time investment and is extremely important.

- **Fencing:** You need to make sure that you have proper fencing not only to constrain the pigs to your premises but to also keep any predators away. A basic 165ft fence will cost you between \$80-\$150 or £50-£75. This will vary based on the type of fence that you choose.

- **Feeder and waterer:** Pigs need a lot of fresh food and water available to them. To feed them, you have the option of a heavy-duty rubber bowl, which will cost about \$25 or £15 each. For waterers, you will need a 55 gallon one at least. The basic cost of this is \$40 or £20.

- **Food:** An adult pig will need about 2.5-3 pounds of food each month to be healthy. This will cost you between \$150-\$200 per month or £75-£100.

- **Bedding:** Pigs will need good bedding material such as straw bales. It will cost you approximately \$5 or £2 for one square bale.

- **Veterinary costs:** Pigs usually only require annual check-ups and vaccinations. This may cost you about \$100-\$300 or £50-150 per year. Each visit can cost you anything between \$30-\$50 or £15-£20.

Only when you are certain that you can manage these ongoing costs should you make an investment in a Kunekune pig. You must not make any compromises on the care of your pet because you are unable to commit financially.

What are the legalities involved with raising pigs?
Like any other pet, you have some legal responsibilities with pigs as well. Some of these laws must be fully understood before you opt for a pet pig, as they may restrict the number of pigs that you can keep. Some laws may not allow you to keep a pet pig in your state at all. Here are some important laws with respect to having pigs.

Travel laws with pigs
When you are travelling with any pet, it is necessary to check the rules of the state or country that you are travelling to. In some states, your pig will need identification that is visible. In some states you need to have a complete blood report to check your pig for brucellosis and other diseases before the pig is allowed to cross the state limit. Some of them may just require a certificate of veterinary inspection or a health certificate.

You need to make sure that you follow these regulations. They are meant to protect not only the pigs in the state that you may be travelling to but your own pig as well. If you are caught violating these rules, the penalties are huge.

We will discuss the travel guidelines for pigs in detail in the following chapters.

Zoning ordinances with respect to pigs

Every state has a different rule when it comes to keeping pet pigs in the city limits. It is possible that some states have conflicting laws in two different cities in the same state. So, you need to make sure that you follow zoning laws that are set by your city to ensure that you are allowed to have one in your city.

There have been several cases in the past where people have brought amendments to zoning laws in their city after bringing a pet pig home. Of course, not everyone is successful and it is definitely not worth the fight and wait.

It is best that you learn the zoning laws before you bring a pig home. You can check the zoning laws with the Agriculture Authorities in your city. Not everyone gets caught with illegally having pigs at home, but when you do, the fines are heavy and the animal could be taken away and in extreme cases, euthanized.

Zoning laws may allow you to keep pigs with certain restrictions such as:

- Number of pigs in each household
- Vaccination requirements
- Limitation with respect to weight

Homeowner's Association Guidelines

You must make sure that you check your HOA guidelines before bringing a pig home. Even this can dictate if you are allowed to have a pig on your property or not. Make sure that you check your HOA paperwork thoroughly if you intend to bring home any kind of pet before you sign them.

Often pigs are not mentioned in these contracts, which could mean that they are either included or excluded. To make sure what the clauses state exactly, you will have to battle it out in court. So, if you plan to bring a pig home, check specifically about the animals that you are allowed to have in the premises.

Personal injury laws

Sometimes accidents happen when you have pets at home. Even the most docile pig can get agitated at times if they are disturbed or spooked. It is possible that the animal responds with a head swipe or with a bite. In any case, you are responsible for your pig's behavior as the owner.

The first responsibility that you have is to make sure that your pig is fully vaccinated. This includes rabies to prevent anything worse from happening from an accidental bite.

If your pig has had a history of bites, make sure that you do not allow him to be around gatherings of unfamiliar people, especially children. You can keep him in a fenced area where he will not be easily bothered.

If your pig has been aggressive, you must place several signs around your property to make sure that everyone who enters is aware that they should stay clear of the animal. Never let children interact with your pig without your permission.

In case your pig is not properly socialized, avoid any community events altogether to be on the safer side.

Property damage laws
This is a very important law for those who are renting a property. Make sure that you take enough pictures of the house and inspect it thoroughly before you move in. If there are any previous damages, note them down and inform the owner prior to moving in.

When you are leaving the house, they may claim that your pig is responsible for damages that existed from the beginning. Also remember that pigs are capable of damaging walls, doors and even floors. They can remove flooring planks just out of boredom sometimes. This may happen in a rented house or in the house of someone that you are visiting. In either case, you are responsible for the damage caused.

Make sure that you keep an eye on your pig when you take them on to someone else's property. Try to bring toys and some food with you to prevent any boredom.

These are the basic laws that you need to be aware of when you decide to bring a pig home. They can prevent unnecessary liabilities in the future and are also necessary to keep your pig safe.

Can they be kept in apartments?
Even though some people do have indoor Kunekune pigs, it is not recommended that you have them in a confined space. They require fresh grass to thrive and do well when they have large pastures to graze on. If you are able to provide your pig with this, then you may consider keeping them indoors. However, apartments are not the ideal setting for a pig. It is recommended that you have indoor pigs if you have an independent house with a large enough yard. When you are keeping pigs indoor, you have to make sure that you take care of the following things:

Provide the pig with a housing area indoors

Your pig will need a small area in your house where they can be confined, especially in the initial days. Crate training is recommended if you are going to keep your pig indoors for a long time. This helps them feel secure and also keeps your property safe from any possible damage.

You do not have to keep the pig in a crate at all times. However, it is recommended that you teach them to be comfortable in one in order to make it easier for you to travel with them or even take them for vet visits.

Kunekune pigs can also become territorial, especially when they are in heat. This is why they need a space that is defined and can become their own. You can choose any part of your house to become the resting and eating place of the pig. You will also have to assign a littering area away from this portion of your house.

Just place a large litter box in the designated area, which is easy for the pig to access. The litter that you use should not be toxic. The best options are pine shavings and dry dirt. Adding a blanket that they can burrow in will also fulfil the foraging needs of your pig.

It is a myth that pigs are messy, unclean creatures. Therefore, you can keep them indoors as long as you have them trained properly.

Litter box training

It is best that your pig has access to some area outdoors where he or she can poop and urinate. However, in very hot conditions or in case of space limitations, this may not always be possible. This makes it necessary for you to have a litter box.

We will talk about litter box training in detail in the following chapter. When you are choosing a litter, there are a few considerations, such as:

- Ensuring that the floor is not slippery and scuffed up. This can lead to injuries when the pig slips and falls, especially if they are under a year old.

- Use a box that does not have any sides. That way, when the pig wants to use it, he will have easy access to it.

- The litter box should ideally fit in a corner as pigs prefer concealed areas to eliminate waste.

Do Kunekune pigs need to be registered?

Before you keep a pet pig at home, you will have to get an identification number from the concerned authority before you do so. This number is used to identify the property that the pigs are reared on. You can apply online for this number.

In some countries, a movement license is required in order to travel with your pig. The details of the same can be obtained from your local Agriculture and Animal Health Authorities.

What is a walking license?
In some countries, such as the UK, you need to have a walking license in order to walk your pig within your premises. You will have to check with the authority corresponding to UK's Animal and Plant Health Agency in your country to obtain the walking license.

You may not be granted a walking license in case the walking area is close to:

- A restaurant
- Pig farm
- Livestock market.

Moving your pigs
You will have to get a tattoo or a tag to identify your pig in case you are moving it away from its regular premises. This marking is also required if you are moving your pig to a show or exhibition, a breeding location or even another country. There are three types of identifiers that are commonly used with pigs:

- Ear tag.
- Slap marks on either side of the front shoulder of the pig with some permanent ink.
- A tattoo on the ear of the animal.

These tags or tattoos are not necessary in piglets that are less than a year old. If you are moving a pig that is less than a year of age, you can use a temporary mark with paint. The mark should last until the pig reaches the destination that you are taking him to.

When moving pig, it is necessary to keep a record of the movement. This is a formal record that must include the following details:

- The full name and address of the person who is maintaining the record
- The date when they pigs were moved
- The identification number
- The number of pigs that were moved
- The address of the area that they were moved from

- The address of the area that the pigs were moved to.

This record should be made in under 36 hours of actually moving the pigs. These records will be examined annually by the concerned authorities. These records must be maintained for at least three years, even if you stop having pigs on your property.

Chapter 3: Bringing a Kunekune Pig Home

Once you are assured that you will be able to provide great care for your pig, you can begin to choose the right sources to bring your pigs home from. The most important part is to ensure that you bring your pig home from a credible source. That will reduce any risk of illnesses or developmental issues in your Kunekune pig.

This chapter will tell you all about the right options to bring your pet home from and also give you tips to help your new pet feel comfortable in your home.

1. Sourcing a Kunekune Pig

When it comes to Kunekune pigs, there are two sources that you can look at. The most common source is a breeder and the other source is an animal shelter where you can adopt a pig from.

Irrespective of the source that you choose, you need to be certain that you are bringing home a pig that is healthy to avoid any unwanted expenses. In addition to that, it can be very difficult for most people to care for a pig with health complications.

There are a few guidelines that will help you pick the perfect source to get your pig from. Learning about the sources and the right way to assess them will help you bring home a healthy Kunekune pig.

Buying from a breeder

There are several farms where Kunekune pigs are bred specifically for selling. A genuine breeder ensures that the pigs are selected carefully and that they are bred in healthy conditions. There are also several commercial breeders who follow unethical measures to produce large numbers of piglets, often leading to unhealthy and sick offspring.

One of the best ways to find a breeder near you is to visit the official website of any Kunekune Pig Association in your country. They often have a list of credited breeders who make pigs to keep as pets and also for breeding and showing purposes.

You may choose to buy piglets or adult pigs depending upon your experience with them. It is always suggested that you bring them home when they are younger to help them blend into your home easily. Older pigs may have some set behavior patterns that will take additional care and training to change.

How do you tell if a breeder is genuine?
There are several observations that you can make when you visit a breeder that will tell you if the breeder is genuine or not. Here are a few points to consider:

- The breeder should be registered with any Kunekune Association in your country. This ensures that they follow the code of ethics laid down by these authorizing bodies.

- The breeder should have a lot of knowledge and should be willing to share that knowledge with you. Any questions that are asked should be met with suitable answers. It is important for the breeder to be willing to spend time with you to answer your queries.

- The breeder should have a screening process for buyers. This ensures that he or she is genuinely concerned about the well-being of the pig.

- The breeder should provide you with several resources that will help you learn about Kunekine pigs before you make a purchase.

- He or she should be willing to have site visits. This will allow potential buyers to assess the conditions that the pigs are bred in. In case you are unable to visit the facility, the breeder should send you all the latest pictures and videos. However, it is highly recommended that you pay a site visit before bringing a pig home.

- The breeder should be willing to take a pig back in case a buyer is unable to keep him for some reason. Any responsible breeder will not allow his or her pig to end up in a shelter. They will also assist in helping the pig find a new home if needed.

- The personality of the breeder should be approachable. They should be willing to allow you to contact them after or before making any purchase.

- The breeder should be willing to give you information about the parent pigs as well. This includes details like the genetics, the health, size, personality, etc. The breeder should seem like he or she interacts with these pigs regularly and actually enjoys being around them.

- They should be willing to show you all the health records of the pig.

- The breeder should be aware of the personality of the piglets. This is a sign that he or she spends enough time with them.

- They should be able to give you references of any previous customers as well as veterinarians.

- The piglets must me spayed or neutered. If the size of the female does not permit spaying, the breeder should have a separate contract for her.

- The breeder should be able to give you all the details that you need about the vaccines including the pros and cons and the possible risks.

- The size and weight expectations that the breeder provides you with should be realistic. Remember that guaranteeing the weight for pigs is not possible. He or she can only give you a height expectation.

- Socializing the pigs is a priority for the breeder.

- The breeder should ask you questions to understand if your family situation is suitable for pigs.

- The pigs should be sent to new homes only when they have started eating solids like pellet feed and not when they are still on milk.

- The website of the breeder should have updated pictures of the pigs, information on health, housing and other needs of the animal. The more transparent the information, the more reliable the breeder.

Questions that you should ask a breeder
Here is a list of questions that you must ask your breeder to understand how genuine he or she is:

- How long have you been breeding Kunekune pigs?

- What is the process used to choose pigs for breeding?

- What is the age of the pig? If the parents are 3-5 years old, then they are fully mature. If the parents are younger than this, it is hard to tell the full growth potential of the piglets.

- Have the parents had any genetic or health issues?

- At what age are the piglets separated from the mother? Do you follow a schedule or do you let the mother decide?

- Are transportation services available across state lines? If so, what veterinary certificates are provided? Have any of these services been used before?

- Are the babies vaccinated or dewormed? Was the mother dewormed before the birth of the piglets?

- Do you offer any other healthcare services before the piglets are sent home?

- Do you offer any type of socializing or training to the piglets before they are sent to their new homes?

- Are the pigs born indoors or outdoors? If they are born outdoors, are they kept inside after weaning to socialize them?

- Are pigs neutered before being sent to new families?

- In case the new family is unable to care for the pig, do you take them back?

- How do you ensure that the pigs have a good quality of life?

- What is the average size of piglets produced by a certain breeding pair?

- Is there any particular type of food that you recommend?

- What is the vaccination schedule that you would recommend?

- Who is the veterinarian that you consult and why have you chosen him or her?

Checking the health of a piglet
There are some giveaway signs to know if the pig is healthy or not. Here are some tips to choose a healthy piglet:

- The piglet should look alert, active and healthy.

- The eyes should be open and free from any discharge or crust.

- The body of the piglet should be rounded and should not have any protruding bones.

- They should not have any signs of illness.

- The pigs must not have any odor and should be clean.

- The bowel movement should be solid and the pig must urinate appropriately.

- The body of the piglet should be proportional without any deformity.

- The hair should be smooth and there should not be any bald patches on the body.

- The skin should not be too dry and must not have any signs of irritation, rashes, bumps or scales.

- The piglets should have been started on solid foods before they are taken to their new homes.

- The piglets should be fully weaned before they are sent to the new home.

- They must be friendly and should not be afraid of human contact.

- The eyes should be bright and clear.

- They must have a healthy gait.

- They should be socialized with the rest of the litter and should not be separated from the mother for 6 weeks at least.

Once the breeder fulfils these conditions, you can make a purchase without any hassle. Make sure that you avoid buying pigs online and make at least one site visit before you choose your pet.

Adopting a pig

The other option that you have when it comes to sourcing pigs is to adopt one. This is the less expensive option. However, you will most often find adult Kunekune pigs for adoption and it is quite likely that the pig has a few behavioral issues that you need to know how to deal with.

With adopted pigs, you need to consider the history of the animal which may, in some cases, also involve abuse and bad treatment. Being the intelligent animals that they are, pigs tend to develop issues with trust or may even be aggressive because of this kind of history.

The good news is that Kunekune pigs are very easy to train, which means that they will respond to any effort that you put in altering a behavior. However, if you do not have any experience with pigs, this may not be the ideal choice for you.

Things to know before adopting a pig

- A pig is not his full size until he is about 3 years old. If you are adopting a pig that is younger than this, be prepared for him to grow more. Please note that we shall refer to the pig as "he" for ease.

- Pigs develop a full adult personality when they are about 2 years old.

- A pig that is adopted will be a little more work than a piglet. With pigs, they do not have any need to please their humans. So, building trust and forging a bond with the animal, especially an adult, is quite a bit of work.

- You need to know as much as you can about the history of the pig before you bring him home. For instance, if you are looking for an indoor pig that is used to living with children, you must find one with a similar history. If the records show that the pig tends to be destructive indoors, you may want to consider having an outdoor setting for him.

- Make sure the pig is checked by a vet before you bring him home. Some diseases can not only be fatal but can also be passed on to human beings.

- Look for someone with pigs to give you advice if you are new to adopting pigs. This will be invaluable while you try to housebreak your new pet.

- If you are bringing home a pair of pigs, especially a male and a female, you may want to consider having them spayed and neutered to be on the safer side.

How to adopt a pig

There are several shelters and farms that rescue pigs that have been abandoned or even abused. You can check with a shelter near you to find out about the best places to adopt pigs from. You can also go online and find places that rescue pigs and check their websites. Here is a detailed adoption process that will tell you what to expect:

- The shelter will check into the zoning laws of your city. Only if you are allowed to keep a pig within your city limits will you be allowed to adopt one.

- You will have to fill out a detailed questionnaire and adoption form that will help them understand your family environment, your lifestyle and also your financial abilities to provide for the pig.

- These shelters list the pigs that are up for adoption on their websites. You will be required to select a maximum of two pigs that you are interested in.

- Once you have selected the pig and your questionnaire is reviewed and found suitable, a meeting is scheduled for you to visit your possible new pet.

- Make sure that you pay at least two visits to understand the personality of your pig before you bring one home.

- Some shelters also offer classes that help you understand pig behavior and will teach you how to deal with issues, if any. It is highly recommended that you attend these classes to learn about your pig. In most cases, these classes are mandatory for adoption.

- Once you have completed your meeting and have taken the required number of classes, a house check is scheduled to ensure that you will be able to provide the necessary environment for the pig to thrive in.

- An adoption fee is collected to reimburse any expenses that have been made for the care of the pig. This is very low in comparison to what you may pay in case you buy a Kunekune pig and varies with each shelter.

- Once the adoption process is complete, you can bring home your new pet pig.

2. Transporting your pig

Whether you choose to bring your pig home from a shelter or from a breeder, you need to make sure that you take the right measures to have your new pet transported to your home.

It is not as simple as putting the pig in the back seat of the car and driving him home. You need to make sure that the animal is comfortable and safe throughout the journey. Here are some useful tips to transport your Kunekune pig.

In case you are crossing state borders

There are some legalities involved if you choose to transport your pig across state borders. Here are some things that you should take care of:

- You need to obtain a health certificate from the breeder or the shelter for your pig. This is a thorough veterinary check to ensure that your pig is not carrying any diseases. If your breeder or shelter does not offer a health certificate, it is a good idea to consider an alternative source to get your pig from altogether. This is an indication that they do not provide any guarantee for the health of the pig. You can also obtain your health certificate from a vet within 72 hours of purchasing the pig.

- This certificate should accompany the pig when he is in transit.

- A health certificate is usually valid for 30 days. However, in some cases, the health check must be done within 10 days of transporting your pig. Make sure you check with the necessary authorities of your country for the correct guidelines.

- In some cases, identification such as a ear tag is mandatory as well.

When you are transporting your pig, make sure you check all the regulations with your Department of Agriculture. Since the rules and regulations change quite often, you have to keep yourself updated. A pig that is travelling without the necessary documents may be confiscated.

Driving your pig to his new home

It does take some time to get your pig used to a car, so it is best that you start when you are paying the initial visits to your pig at the breeder's or at the shelter.

Some pigs are extremely calm when they travel and others may be very nervous. There are chances that your pig will even have accidents in the car if he is afraid, so make sure you have enough substrate and material to clean up after him. Here are some tips that you can follow to transport your pig:

- Do not place the pig on the lap of a passenger if you are travelling with one. This will only make him more nervous.

- It is best to transport your pig in a crate. Make sure that it is lined with enough substrate such as newspaper that is absorbent in case your pig has an accident.

- Using puppy pads inside the crate will also help your pig stay safe inside the crate.

- Keep the temperature of the air conditioner lower than room temperature to make sure that your pig does not overheat.

- It is also a good idea to cover the windows if it is a hot day to prevent any heat stroke.

- If it is a long journey, stop every 20-30 minutes to check on your pig. Make sure you give him ample water to prevent any chances of dehydration or salt toxicity.

- The crate must be secure in the backseat. It is a good idea to take the backrest down to make more space for your pet.

- Do not play any loud music and try to keep the environment calm and composed for the pig.

- In case your pig seems to get car sick, you can give him some ginger root to chew on as a remedy.

When you make your visits to the breeder or the animal shelter, get your pig in the car for a while and drive for about 15-20 minutes. This will help you understand how the pig responds to being driven around and will help you prepare in advance. If your pig is extremely motion sick, a vet can prescribe medication to relax the animal and prevent any form of stress.

3. Your pig's first day at home

Kunekune pigs are extremely friendly for the most part. However, when you bring your pet home for the first time, it is very important to keep realistic expectations from your new pet. This is a new place for him and he is probably nervous about the new scents and sights.

Give your pig some time to get accustomed to these changes. It is best that you take it slow when it comes to introducing him to his new home. The more you force your affection on him, the harder it is going to get for him to get used to it.

What to expect in the first few days

- The pig may be scared and jumpy.

- Even a pig that has been socialized and is used to being handled will take some time to get used to you.

- Be prepared to give your new pet a lot of attention and space at the same time.

- It may take your pig about 3 days to warm up to you. In the case of older pigs it may take longer and even several weeks.

- Once the pig is used to you, he will follow you wherever you go.

- The pig may even try to run away in some cases. So make sure that you never leave him in a place that is not enclosed.

Making your pig feel at home

There are some things that you can do to make your pig more comfortable in the first few days of arriving in his new home. Here are some things to keep in mind to make this phase easier for you and your pig:

- **The first few days make all the difference:** It is really exciting to bring home a pet pig. You will spend the first few days just understanding the personality of your pig. Pigs are very curious and this makes this phase even more interesting. If you are able to get the first few interactions right, you will set the tone for a lifetime of trust and love.

- **Pigs will not trust immediately:** With other pets like dogs, it is possible that they warm up to and even approach you instantly. The bonding process is a little longer in the case of pigs. If you have rescued a pig, then this time will probably be longer. However, if you are able to make enough time and put in some effort, the body that is formed is simply incredible.

- **Have realistic expectations:** Your pig may squeal every time you approach him, let alone pick him up or pet him. The focus for the first few days should be on the basic needs of the pig. Make sure that he has enough food and water and a quiet place to rest. Always call the pig to you and never approach him off guard. Pet and cuddle with your pig only as often as he will let you. This will help him trust you slowly and get comfortable when he is handled by you.

- **Don't get frustrated:** Even when you give him all the treats in the world and spoil him silly, he will seem completely indifferent. This can be frustrating to many new pet parents. However, when your pig is ready, he will come to you on his own. This will just happen out of the blue one day. You just need to keep at it and try everything that you can to warm up to your beloved new pet.

- **Warming up to your pet pig:** It is absolutely natural for a pig to not let you touch or pet him on the first day. He may not let you do this for several days, in fact. Sit on the floor, place a few treats and allow the pig to approach you. When he allows you to, give him gentle scratches behind the ear. You know your pig is completely comfortable when he will allow you to give him a belly rub. Spend as much time doing this as you can and he will begin to feel safe in your presence.

- **Don't rush interactions with friends and family:** When you bring home a pet pig, it is natural for your friends and family to be just as excited as you to meet him. Some of them may even try to hold the pig, which may set off an episode of screaming. Make sure that you tell them to let the pig approach them and not vice versa. Many of them may even be disapproving of your pig's behavior, but this is a natural process and you must never lose faith in your little friend. Unlike dogs, pigs will not greet people happily. They may not even want to meet anyone initially. This doesn't mean that the pig is unfriendly. It only means that he is taking his time to get used to the new people and his brand new environment.

When you see that your pig feels safe and happy around you, you will realize that it is absolutely worth the wait. Just don't allow yourself to get too overwhelmed and stay patient.

4. Introducing a Kunekune to your family

Your family should follow all the steps mentioned above when it comes to interacting with the pig for the first few days. Now, your family may include little children or other pets like cats, dogs or other pigs. Understanding the general behavior of pigs will help you make these introductions much easier.

Kunekune pigs and kids

Kunekune pigs have a generally docile personality, which makes them perfect for a home with children. Children should be taught to interact correctly with the pig, keeping the first few interactions distant and relaxed. Make sure you teach the children not to approach the pig when he is not ready.

However, it is best that you bring home the pig only when you have older kids. With children who are too young, Kunekune pigs can be dominant and sometimes, pushy. We will discuss later in this chapter about the dominant nature of Kunekune pigs to help you make their introductions to the rest of your family more positive and safe.

Kunekune pigs and cats

Most Kunekune pig owners will agree that these animals get along best with cats. Cats seem to love to cuddle up with pigs and often use them as their own little pillows. Pigs, on the other hand, seem to be indifferent to cats and will not really mind them being around. In some cases, however, pigs have been noted to be very playful with cats. They will simply lay down when cats rub their bodies against them. Of all the other pets, cats are the best companions that you can find for your Kunekune pigs.

Kunekune pigs and dogs

There are several instances when Kunekune pigs get along really well with dogs. However, to keep your pig safe, it is best that you never leave them by themselves without any supervision.

By natural order, dogs are predators and pigs are prey animals. If your pig does something to upset the dog, there are chances of an attack. In most cases, it has been found that a fight between a pig and a dog is initiated by the former. If you have a dog as a pet, here are a few things that you should keep in mind:

- Dogs are naturally quite tolerant towards pigs. However, sometimes habits of pigs, like screaming, can really set the dog off. It is worse because pigs do not back off easily and may ask for a lot of trouble.

- You must never feed your Kunekune pig and a dog close to one another. Most fights stem from them trying to eat each other's food.

- If you are going to be away, your pig and dog should be kept in separate enclosures.

- It is not necessary for the pig to be bitten or attacked by a dog. Sometimes a dog may chase a pig around for so long that the pig may even have a fatal case of overheating.

Kunekune pigs and other pigs

It is always advised that you bring home pigs in pairs. This is because they are naturally herd animals. Pigs need one another in order to feel safe. They also love having companions that they can eat, play and sleep with. Pigs make great companions for each other. In fact, having other pigs around can actually keep your pig mentally and physically stimulated.

If you are unable to give your pig enough time and attention, getting him a piggy companion is a wonderful idea. When they are bored and alone, pigs tend to become depressed and may even develop behavioral issues and health issues.

Making sure that you introduce them correctly is necessary. In the beginning, keeping them in neighboring enclosures is the best option, as it will reduce any injury as a result of dominance games or even aggression in some rare cases.

Dominant behavior in pigs

Before you introduce your Kunekune pig to other animals, you must note that they often display dominant behavior. A pig may challenge another animal or even humans at times.

When they are challenging someone, they tend to lunge or nip. They may even give them a head swipe or simply nudge them for some attention. These are called dominance games that pigs even play with each other. If you find your pig nudging you and you simply move away, it indicates to him that he is now the boss.

One of the best ways to prevent this behavior is to stop the pig from nudging you or entering your personal territory. You can do this with the

45

use of a stick that sets boundaries. When the pig tries to nudge you, block him with a stick.

If the pig backs off, make sure that you reward him by rubbing his belly and giving him some treats. Using the stick as an extension of your body will give the impression that you are larger than you actually are. This makes the pig back off and understand your space.

Dominant behavior is natural in herd animals. They use this to determine who the leader of the group will be. Like any other prey animal, they need a leader to their herd. The leader is responsible for showing the rest of the herd the different places to sleep, drink or eat. The leader keeps the herd safe. Even at home, your pig needs a leader in order to feel safe.

Chapter 4: Caring for your Kunekune Pig

Like any other pet, there are some basic requirements of pigs that you need to fulfill in order to keep them happy and feeling safe. Providing good care requires you to mentally and physically stimulate your pig and also ensure that he feels safe in your home.

This chapter will tell you everything that you need to know about making sure that your pig is happy and healthy.

1. Housing requirements of pigs

Some pig owners may be open to the idea of keeping their pigs indoors. However, if you want to keep your pig outdoors, you need to make sure that you provide proper shelter to your pig to keep them safe from heat and rain. You also need to remember that pigs are very sensitive to heat and cold and may develop serious health issues if they do not have proper shelter.

Location of the housing area

- The housing area should be elevated to ensure that no water is retained when it rains. It also prevents any flooding of the housing area.

- The housing area should have some shaded areas around it.

- It should also have the availability of a good amount of fresh air.

- It should be kept at a distance from your home.

- Make sure that the housing area is easy to access.

- It should have a good manure disposal option and must be connected to good electricity and water sources.

The temperature of the housing area

Temperature plays a vital role in the well being of pigs. They are extremely sensitive to temperature fluctuations and may develop serious health issues. Here is what you need to know about the temperature of the housing area:

- You need to make sure that the temperature inside the housing area can be controlled to ensure that the pigs are not too hot or too cold. The production of heat in the pig's body should not depend on the air temperature. It must depend instead on the weight and the feeding habits of the pig.

- If your pigs are huddled together, it is a sign that they are too cold. They may even shiver in this case.

- If the pigs are keeping away from their companions or even urinate within the pen, they may be too warm. If the breath of the pig is fast and he breathes more than 50 times each minute, it means that he is too hot.

- The temperature at which pigs need to cool off their bodies by wallowing or with water sprays is called evaporative critical temperature.

- The temperature that is most tolerable to the pig is called the upper critical limit and the lowest tolerable temperature is called lower critical limit.

- To keep the pig warm, make sure that there are not cracks in the wall or near the floor. Avoid any trenches that are open ended. Have covers and boxes that the pig can crawl into when he is too cold.

- The housing area should be kept dry. For this reason, using substrate like wood shavings or straw is recommended as long as they are cleaned out regularly and kept dry.

- To keep the pig cool, have small pits or pools around the housing area that they can wallow in when they are feeling too warm.

Insulation and ventilation of housing area

- Irrespective of the environment, you need to ensure that the housing area has ample fresh air.

- Fresh air is needed to keep the moisture, dust, bacteria and any odor out of the housing area.
- All the sources of ventilation are also responsible for reducing the temperature of the housing area, so make sure that you have some form of insulation available as well.

- Keeping the roof and the walls insulated will prevent any loss or gain of heat. Also make sure that the housing area is draft proof.

- You can provide insulation with the help of any vapor barrier. This makes sure that the inner lining of the housing area is protected and also prevents any moisture.

- Any source of ventilation should be built in a way that allows you to control the direction of airflow. That way, it does not fall directly on the pigs.

Construction of the housing area

You can use material such as wood or even carbon fiber to construct the housing area of your pig. You must remember that the material that you use should not trap heat or emanate any heat. The lighter the material, the better. Here are some tips to construct a good housing area for your pig:

- The floor size should be at least 3mx3m per pig.

- The housing area should be elevated and should be at least 60 centimeters above ground level.

- There must be a gap of at least 2cms between the floor boards of the housing area.

- The roof should be constructed such that it allows some sunlight in through one side. It should also provide complete shade in some part of the housing area.

- The house should lie on the east west axis, lengthwise to make sure that it is protected from any rain or sun.

Feeder and waterers

If you have just one pig as a pet, this is not really much of a concern, as you can use a regular bowl to provide water to your pet. However, in case you have multiple pigs living in each housing area, you need to take enough care to ensure that they have enough food and water. They should also have their own personal space when eating or drinking to prevent any fights. Here are some tips to give your Kunekune pigs proper access to food and water:

- You can use wet and dry feeders as long as you do not have more than 10 pigs per feeder.

- When you use troughs make sure that each pig has at least 0.3 meters of space for himself at the trough.

- Pigs must always have ample access to clean and good quality water to drink.

- When it gets hotter, you can increase the number of drinkers when you have more than one pig.

- For younger pigs, using a bite type drinker is the best option to prevent the bowl from over turning.

- The drinkers should always be placed over slat. That way, when the slat becomes wet, pigs are encouraged to use slat even to urinate and poop on.

Cleaning the housing area
The housing area should always be kept clean and dry. This ensures that no microbes that cause serious health issues to pigs can thrive in the housing area. It is best to change the substrate as soon as it becomes damp. As for the routine cleaning, it is best that you clean the housing area thoroughly at least once a week. Here is a step by step process to help you clean the housing area easily:

- Remove any feeders and waterers or other equipment.

- The loose dung should be removed from the floor and possibly the wall of the housing area.

- The wall and the ceiling should be hosed down to remove any dust. Soak the floor with soapy water.

- If the housing area is heavily caked, you should keep it soaked for at least 24 hours. Soaking makes it easier to clean the housing area.

- Then hose down the shelter with hot water. If there is any adjacent housing area, make sure that the pigs housed there are protected, too.

- The floor, walls and the roof should be disinfected using a spray. This helps remove any fungi, bacteria or virus from the housing area. It is best that you clean the housing area thoroughly before using any disinfectant to make it more effective.

- The water system should be disinfected.

- Any weed or grass should be removed fully to prevent mice, rats or flies from entering the area.

In order to keep the housing area clean, you need to make sure that there is a good drainage system in place within the pen. You must return the pigs to the housing area only when it is fully dry.

2. What to feed Kunekune pigs

Good nutrition is the key to having happy and healthy pets. You must make sure that you understand all the nutritional requirements of your pet to prevent any related health conditions or issues.

Dietary requirements of Kunekune pigs

The dietary requirements of an adult Kunekune pig are as follows:

- 1-1.5 kilos of food
- More fiber than regular commercial pigs
- High protein
- At least 5 liters of water each day and more if the weather is warmer and if the pig is lactating.

It is often said that these animals can survive off grass alone. However, studies have revealed that only certain types of grasses are capable of providing them with the necessary amount of protein.

When they are fed 1500grams of grass hay, they only get 10% of protein and 33% of fiber. This can cause a lot of discomfort to the pig, as it is not enough nutrients. Even with alfalfa grass, they only get 13% of protein and about 38% of fiber.

The good thing about Kunekune pigs is that they are extremely hardy animals and will require very little supplementation in their diet. According to the British Kunkune Society, a mixture of weaner meal and 16% sow meal along with grass pellets is a good idea. Grass pellets should be soaked in water and given to the pigs only when fresh grass is not available. This provides the animal with a more balanced diet that contains the necessary amount of protein and fiber.

Kunekune pigs are extremely fond of nuts and fruits. This can be given to the pig in moderation as a supplement to get important vitamins and minerals. However, it is necessary that you account for any additional calories in the diet because of these foods to prevent issues like obesity in the pigs.

You must make sure that your pig gets more calories when the weather is colder or when the pig is either pregnant or lactating. The diet should be changed accordingly to ensure that your pig gets good nutrition.

Keeping an eye on the body condition of the pig will help you understand whether he is overfed or underfed. In case your pig seems to be gaining excessive weight, you can reduce the food intake to 1000 grams per day. If the pig seems to be losing weight excessively, you can increase it to 1500 grams each day.

Why grass is important

It is extremely important for your Kunekune pigs to have ample grazing area in order to thrive. They should have a good amount of grass to graze all through the year. It is recommended that your pig has at least 5-6 acres of land to graze on.

One thing to note is that pigs use the grass not only to feed but also to walk on and play on. It is also possible that the land gets divided during wet weather. This is why you need to have a separate grazing area that is separated using an electric fence or pig wire. Pigs should be kept in the housing area when the weather is wet to make sure that the grazing period lasts longer.

Grass is important for a lot of reasons. Foraging gives the pigs great mental stimulation. In addition to that, pigs that are grass fed get two to five times the necessary nutrients, especially conjugated linoleic acid and omega-3 fatty acids.

Omega-3 fatty acids, when digested, are stored as compounds that are anti-inflammatory. Omega-6, on the other hand, is stored as compounds that are inflammatory. Both are equally important for the pig's body and should be well balanced.

Pigs should not consume excessive omega-6 fatty acids, as they can lead to excessive inflammation in the body. There are several sources of these fatty acids such as grains, nuts and vegetable oil. Therefore, these foods must only be provided in moderation to keep the pig healthy.

Processed foods will contain a high amount of Omega-6 fatty acids, as they are rich in corn oil and soy. To strike a balance, pigs need a good source of Omega-3 fatty acids, which is commonly found in grass. For this reason, pigs that usually consume grass have a higher content of Omega-3 in their body.

Another type of important fatty acid is conjugated linoleic acid. This, too, has anti-inflammatory properties, which can prevent several health issues including cancer. CLA is obtained through grass and is higher in animals that are grass fed.

In addition to the above, grass is also a good source of Vitamins B, E and beta-carotene, which have several health benefits for pigs. These nutrients are also vital in preventing major health conditions that commonly affect pigs.

What you should never feed Kunekune pigs
Here are some foods that you should never feed your pig:

- Table scraps of human food
- Meat
- Bones
- Blood
- Eggs
- Egg shells
- Kitchen refuse that may have meat in them.

3. Seasonal care for pigs
As mentioned above, Kunekune pigs are very sensitive to temperature changes. As a result, you must make sure that you provide your pig with appropriate care with changing weather. This means that summer care for Kunekune pigs is quite different from winter care.

Summer care for Kunekune pigs
You need to take a lot of care in warmer months, as pigs tend to suffer from several health issues. The heat tends to put a lot of strain on these animals. Pigs do not have any way of releasing the heat from the body, except for wallowing or soaking themselves in water.

It is not enough to use fans or air conditioning either, as the chance of pigs getting too cold arises. Then you will have to provide them with a blanket to snuggle up into.

Here are some key tips to keep in mind when the warmer months approach:

- **Never leave your pet in a vehicle:** This rule applies to just about any pet that you may have such as a cat or a dog. In the summer heat, leaving a pig unattended in the car is completely prohibited. They are at risk of suffering from heat stroke within minutes of being left in the car. This can lead to severe issues like brain damage and can even be fatal.

- **Provide them with a lot of fresh water:** During the warmer months, pigs need more water. Make sure that they have access to cool and clean drinking water at all times.

- **Ensure that they have enough shade:** Both indoors and outdoors, pigs should have access to enough shade to keep themselves cool. This may include specially constructed shelters or even trees.

- **Be careful when you are outdoors:** You must ensure that your pig is never allowed to go outdoors in the middle of the day. This is when the sun is harshest. If it is a particularly hot day, it is best that you keep your pet indoors all day.

- **Look for bug bites:** The chances of a tick or flea infestation is highest during summer. Make sure that your pig is not showing any signs of allergies due to bug bites or stings either.

- **Give the pig water to wallow in:** If you have a pool, allow your pig some pool time. You can also fill up kiddie pools with water and let your pigs wallow in it. When your pig is near any water source, make sure you keep an eye on him or her to prevent any chances of drowning.

Winter care for Kunekune pigs

Winters can be just as harsh as summers for pigs. Just because Kunekune pigs have fur on their body, it does not mean that they are protected from the cold. You need to take the following measures to ensure that your pig does not get too cold:

- **Keep the pig warm:** If you commonly keep your Kunekune pigs outdoors, you need to make sure that they have an insulated shelter to seek warmth in. If the pig is normally indoors, you need to make sure that he has a blanket that can keep him warm. Some pet owners also purchase specially designed sweaters for their Kunekune pigs.

- **Ensure that the pig is kept dry:** Colder months can be accompanied by snow or rain. If your pig gets wet, make sure that you dry him immediately. The hooves should also be kept dry, as they can develop cracks and cuts because of the cold weather.

- **Give them access to water:** It may seem like your pig does not need as much water during winters. Quite contrary to that, pigs are at as much risk of dehydrating during winters as they are during the warmer months.

- **Make sure that that your pig is away from heat sources:** It is common for pigs to want to snuggle up near a fireplace or near a heater. These heat sources can burn the skin of the pig and should, therefore, be kept away from them.

- **Beware of holiday plants:** Come winter and it is time for holiday plants such as mistletoe or a Christmas tree. The needles from the Christmas tree can harm your pig. In addition to that, some of the other holiday plants can actually be toxic for pigs. It is best to keep your pig away from them.

In addition to taking seasonal precautions, you need to provide your pig with the best possible care all year round. This makes sure that they get nothing but the best and that they are happy all year round.

4. Grooming Kunekune pigs

Keeping your Kunekune pigs clean takes you one step closer to keeping them disease free. If you are keeping your pet indoors, especially, you need to make sure that he is clean and tidy.

Grooming is also a very important bonding activity for pet pigs and their owners. Here are some grooming activities that are important to keep your Kunekune pig looking fresh and clean.

Bathing your Kunekune pig

Quite contrary to popular belief, Kunekune pigs are very clean creatures. They love to keep themselves clean by wallowing in mud and in water. However, you may bathe your pig if you are keeping him indoors or if he has any dirt or debris on his body.

It is important to note that Kunekune pigs do not have any body odor naturally. This is because their skin is naturally dry and does not produce as many oils as other pets like dogs or cats. If your pig smells foul, be sure to check his environment and get your pig checked for any skin or health issues.

Bathing a pig is quite easy and here is a step by step process of getting your pig used to bath time and ensuring that he enjoys it:

- In general, pigs are very fond of water. However, in some cases, they may be alarmed by the sound of running water from the tap or the water hose.

- The first step is to familiarize your pig with a bath set up. Bathing a pig in a tub is the best option to keep him calm.

- Place a rubber mat inside the tub or the sink to make sure that the pig does not slip. Fill it with water up to a few inches. Make sure that the water is warm.

- Float some of your pig's favorite treats such as lettuce or cheerios in the water and let the pig into the tub. Let the pig take his time to become accustomed to the water. He will also be calm because he has his treats to nibble on.

- Using a brush or a plastic scrubber, rub the body of the piglet gently. If the body language of the pig is comfortable and relaxed, you can move on to applying the shampoo.

- Use shampoos that are recommended for pigs always. Good examples are Ultra shampoo and Micro-mist, which ensure that the skin of the pig does not become too dry. Any other shampoo like cat or dog shampoo will strip the pig's skin of natural oils.

- Before you apply the shampoo, make sure that you remove all the treats from the water.

- Lather up the shampoo well and scrub the body to remove any possible dead skin. Rinse your pig's body using a plastic cup. Usually the water that comes out after rinsing is very dirty. Clean the tub out and refill it with cold water.

- Using a hose or a faucet is advised only after your pig is used to his bath time to avoid spooking him.

Make sure that you give your pig a bath only when it is absolutely necessary. Over bathing will make the skin extremely dry. Never apply any oil on to your pig's skin. This will retain all the dirt and debris and will also promote the growth of bacteria and parasites on the skin of the pig. This will lead to a foul smell from the pig's body.

Hoof care for Kunekune pigs

Keeping the hooves of the pig trimmed prevent them from cracking and breaking. In some pigs, you may have to trim the hooves more frequently than others. There are several contributing factors such as the conformation of the pig, the substrate used in the housing area and the exercise that the pig gets. For instance, if the pasture has hard packed clay or dirt, then the hooves do not have to be trimmed as frequently. However, if the pig lives indoors and usually walks on softer surfaces, trimming should be done more frequently.

When you see that the nails of the hooves curve inwards, it is an indication that they need to be trimmed. If they curve in too much, then it can cause locomotive damage or structural damage to the pig.

If you do not have enough experience with pigs, you can have the hooves trimmed by a vet. However, you can also do it at home as you gain more experience with your beloved pet. Here is a step by step process of trimming the hoof of your pig:

- Make sure that your pig is bonded enough with you to trust you to allow hoof trimming. This may take some time. You must never simply grab the legs and try to trim the hoof.
- Start by sitting down near your pig and giving him a good belly rub. Then, place your hand on his leg or hoof and massage it gently. If the pig yanks his foot away, then try again another day. If he lets you hold his leg, you can try to move on to the next step.

- You have special hoof nippers that should only be used when you have enough experience handling pigs. If you are new to this, it is best that you use a nail file that is normally used for acrylic nails or even a wood file.

- Take it slow when you are trimming the hooves of your pig. Do not force or rush him into this, as it will only make him more wary.

- Make a note of the quick, which provides the blood supply to the hoof. The darker area on the hoof comprises of the quick. You must be sure not to nick this, as it may cause bleeding.

- You can use styptic powder to prevent excessive bleeding. If the hoof does bleed, make sure that you stop and then continue the next day.

Unless the pad has been cut or the nail has been ripped off, this will heal itself.

- Hold one leg at a time while your pig is on his side and gently file the hoof. If the pig gets edgy, continue when he is more comfortable.

Cleaning the ear of the Kunekune pig

Just like dogs or cats, pigs develop waxy dirt in the ear that appears flaky and brown. If the ears are not cleaned regularly, they may become infected. However, you must never use any liquid cleaner, as it increases the chances of disease and infection. It can also lead to a permanent head tilt in younger pigs.

The best option is to use a cotton swab or gauze to clear this waxy deposit. Just make sure that the loose debris does not fall down the ear canal. Again, when it comes to ear cleaning, you need to be certain that your pig trusts you a 100%. It is not necessary to get all the debris out at once.

Trimming the tusk of a Kunekune pig

Both male and female Kunekune pigs have tusk that protrude from the upper jaw. In the case of females, these tusks are much smaller and do not protrude in most cases. However, with males, they can become really large and can also be dangerous to you and your family if the pig develops any behavioral issues or shows instances of dominant behavior.

Tusks should only be trimmed if they are causing health issues or are dangerous for you. Overgrown tusks can cause issues like sores or cuts in the gums of the animal. This is when they need to be maintained and trimmed.

The tusk is a part of the jawbone and should be trimmed very carefully. It is never recommended to do this at home. A part of the tusk should always be left behind, preferably about ½ inch. If you trim it too close, it will lead to some serious infections. Therefore, always take your pet to the vet to have his tusk trimmed so that they are not overgrown and hazardous.

Chapter 5: Training Kunekune Pigs

Training your Kunekune pig is a lot of fun. It is also a great way to bond with your pig. Intelligent animals like Kunekune pigs require a lot of mental stimulation. With these training sessions, you can enrich your pig's mental abilities. Of course, the basics of training such as housebreaking and behavior training are quite necessary to make sure that your pig is suitable to keep at home as a pet.

1. Housebreaking your pig

If you are keeping your pig indoors then you can train him to use a litter box. You can fashion a special litter box for your pig with a carton or a cement-mixing box. Just make sure that you have one side open to allow easy access.

Line the litter box with pine shavings. You must never use cedar shavings or any kind of kitty litter. This type of substrate usually has oils in it and may even clump together. If the pig ingests this accidentally, it can lead to severe intestinal blockages.

The litter box should be placed in any area that is far away from the sleeping area of your pig. Make sure that once your litter box location is fixed you do not change it, as pigs do not like to change their potty areas.

Placing a few droppings, often called "pig berry", in the litter box can urge the pigs to use it to do their business. Every day, allow the pig to walk around the litter box a few minutes first thing in the morning, immediately after feed and before bedtime. Pigs are creatures of habit and will eventually learn to use the litter box. Until the age of 6 months, do not be too harsh on your pig as they have not developed the necessary muscles to control these bodily functions.

You can also walk your pig to the litter box every two hours initially. Note the timings when he is most likely to poop and take him to the litter box at the same time each day. Pigs are extremely intelligent and will, sooner or later, figure out what you are expecting of them.

Training your pig to potty outdoors

If you do not really want to have a litter box indoors, you can also train your pig to do his business outdoors. Follow all the steps mentioned above. The only thing that you will change is that you will take the pig outdoors every two hours in the initial training period.

Just let your pig play outdoors and make a note of the potty timings. The more consistently you take him out at these times, the better are the chances of him developing a good habit of using the outdoor space to do his business.

2. Basic Obedience training

In general, obedience training is a great way to bond with your pig. It is especially important when you plan on showing your pig. The basic commands to teach your pigs are sit, spin, stay and shake hooves. It is quite easy to train pigs as they respond very well to training.

Sit

- Hold your pig's favorite treat above his head and say the word "sit".

- Lift it up until the pig is forced to sit down, as he cannot tilt his head any further.

- Give him the treat and shower him with appreciation.

- If he continues to sit in the position for more than 10 seconds, give him another treat.

- After a few attempts, the pig will respond to just the vocal command.

Spin

- All you have to do is hold the treat in front of your pig and let him follow it in a circle.

- As you start doing this say the word, "Spin".

- If your pig completes one full circle, give him a treat.

- Repeat this until the pig responds solely to the voice command.

Shake hooves

- Once your pig has mastered the sit command, you can move on to this one.

- Sit in front of your pig and say the word "Shake".

- When you do so, gently pick up his paw and hold it in your hand.

- Then repeat the vocal command. If the pig gives you his paw voluntarily, reward him with a treat.

Stay

- This is the hardest trick of all to teach your pig.

- Pigs tend to do whatever they like to and will follow you around even when you ask them to stay.

- The best time to practice this is during meals.

- Hold the food bowl in your hand and ask the pig to sit. Then say the command, "stay" and back up one step.

- If the pig stays, you can put the food bowl down.

- Increase the number of steps that you back up to make this more challenging for the pig.

3. Behavioral Training

Aggression is the most common behavioral issue with pigs. They will show very obvious signs of aggression. Learning to deal with aggression as early as possible is a must to make sure that you do not have any accidents or bites, which can be quite severe in the case of pigs.

Signs of aggression in pigs

- Head swipes
- Upright Mohawk
- Barking
- Charging
- Grunting
- Side stepping with Mohawk raised.

'Move the pig' training

To curb aggressive behavior it is extremely important to show them that you are the boss or the leader. Move the pig is a popular training method that is used to deal with aggressive pigs.

- Make sure that your pig is entirely calm when you are practicing this method. The room should not have any distractions and noises.

- Step towards your pig in an authoritative manner and make a hand movement or a gesture while saying the words "Let's go". It should indicate urgency but should not seem like you are yelling. You can even make a sound like an urgent clap.

- The pig should feel like something is happening and should become alert.

- Even if the pig gets up and takes two steps away from you, stop the signal and show your appreciation with a belly rub or with the words, "good boy" or "good girl".

This should become a habit so that if you see signs of any aggression in your pig, saying the words "Let's Go" should be enough to distract him. If your pig is overly aggressive, use a sorting board in front of you when you are approaching him.

Chapter 6: Breeding Kunekune Pigs

Sows can be bred twice a year. They will have 7-10 piglets each time. The litter is also known as a farrow or a shoat. Female pigs that have already delivered a litter are called a sow.

An intact male pig is known as a boar. If he has sired a litter, he is said to be proven. A female pig that has not delivered a litter yet is called a gilt. They are fertile at the age of 10 months and the boars become fertile when they are 12 months old.

It is advised, however, that you wait until the gilt is 1-1.5 years of age before you actually breed her. There are several farrowing problems that crop up when they are bred earlier than this age.

By this age, the body of the pig is fully mature and she is capable of having piglets.

1. Pairing kunekune pigs

If you plan to breed Kunekune pigs, it is a good idea to pay some attention to their bloodlines. This helps you understand how the offspring will possibly be.

Although Kunekune pigs are quite common these days, it is still hard to find suitable pairs. Often the pairs are very closely related to one another. This is why most breeders list pigs under the bloodline of both the mother and the father. Each bloodline has a unique appearance and personality. Knowing about them helps you understand what to expect from the offspring.

Preparing for the litter

Kunekune pigs are slower to grow, that is why they are sexually mature a lot later. It is best that you keep the male and female separated when they reach puberty so that they will breed when you actually want them to and not earlier.

You must have the gilt checked by a vet thoroughly before you breed her. She needs to have all the necessary vaccinations to ensure that she does not pass on any illnesses to the offspring. She should be completely dewormed. You should also check her weight to make sure that she is in best health to breed.

Kunekune pigs need ample water and food to ensure that she is able to sustain the period of pregnancy. They gestation period is for 3 months, 3 weeks and 3 days. This is when you should prepare the furrowing quarters for the pig.

Preparing the furrowing quarters
In order to furrow the babies, the mother will require a warm and draft-free space. If the pig is furrowing in the colder months, you need to have heat lamps available to warm up the part of the housing area that gets cold. Automatic lamps are available to detect the temperature of the room and turn off or turn on accordingly.

The furrowing area should have pig rails that will allow the piglets to escape in case the mom is about to step on them or lay on them accidentally. Piglets love to go to heat lamps when they are cold and will go to mom in order to eat. It is a good idea to hang the heat lamps away from the mom's resting area to attract the piglets and prevent them from getting crushed.

Farrowing
Farrowing is the process of giving birth. You need to take your pregnant gilt to the veterinarian for a final round of booster shots about 5 weeks before the due date. This keeps the babies immune from any health conditions.

When the pig is close to furrowing, she will begin to dig and paw in the bedding material. She will try to make a nest that almost looks like a large bowl. The vulva begins to swell and the teats of the pig become elongated. When you place your hands on the side of the stomach, you will also feel the babies turning and kicking.

Wiping the pig with a damp cloth will cool her off and will also remove any debris from her body. Each piglet will come out on its own. What is fascinating is that these pigs come out of the birthing sack and will also have the cords cut. You can pick up each of the pigs and wipe them off completely to keep them clean.

You can even let it dry off so that you do not interfere with the birthing process. In just a few moments after being born, piglets are able to walk and sometimes, even run.

Once the mom has finished delivering the babies, the after birth is released. This is when the whole farrowing process is fully over. In very rare conditions will the mom have more piglets after the after birth.

Kunekune pigs make wonderful moms and will even call out to the little ones to feed them. They even make soft grunting noises when feeding the babies. It almost seems like she is singing to them while they feed.

Chapter 7: Healthcare of Kunekune Pigs

Healthcare is one of the biggest responsibilities of a pet owner. The first step is to make sure that you prevent any disease or illness in your pet. Identifying an illness in your pet is also crucial to prevent the condition from becoming severe, and in some cases, incurable.

This chapter tells you all that you need to know about providing perfect healthcare for your Kunekune pigs. From preventive care and theidentification of common illnesses to the treatment options for these illnesses, you will get all the information that you require before you bring home a Kunekune pig.

1. Identifying illnesses in Kunekune pigs

Early identification is one of the key factors to keeping your pig in good health. If you have a group of pigs as pets, it is a good idea to check them regularly for any illnesses. There are several visual cues and also cues from touch and smell that you can get when it comes to identifying illnesses in your Kunekune pigs.

Although it is recommended that you check your pigs on a daily basis, once you learn these cues, you will be able to tell even with your daily interactions with your pet. You will not have to do a clinical examination everyday if you are observant and sensitive to the smallest changes.

Visual cues of illness

- You will see the pig lose his appetite slowly. While this is easy to detect in animals that are housed, it is harder when you have a large free ranging group. When you see a sudden drop of appetite in your pigs, the first thing to do would be to check the water sources of the animals. If they have ample water, then lack of appetite is a sign of disease.

- Dull appearance and listlessness is a sign of early stages of illnesses in pigs.

- Raising of the body hair and shivering could be a sign of meningitis or any infection of the joints. This is normally seen in younger pigs.

- Loss of body weight could be an indication of several health issues including dehydration, pneumonia and diarrhea.

- Any nasal discharge or discharge around the eyes is a sign of respiratory infections. Excessive salivation is also an indication of rare conditions like vesicular disease. In the case of sows, it is important to watch out for any discharge from the vulva as it could indicate endometritis, cystitis or vaginitis.

- Mucous, blood or any other change in the fecal discharge is a sign of various diseases of the gastrointestinal tract. Constipation is another important indicator of disease in pigs.

- Look for any changes in the skin of the animal. Issues like lesions are an indication of viral or bacterial infections commonly.

- If you see that the respiration rate in the animal has changed, make sure you take him to the vet immediately. The type of breathing abnormality, whether it is short or deep with excessive movement of the chest, is related to the type of diseases that your pig could be carrying.

Observing a group of pigs
If you have more than one pig at home, you should check them collectively for any signs of illnesses. Here are some things that you should take note of. They also include the condition of the living area besides the obvious symptoms in the pig:

- The temperature of the housing area
- A sudden increase in the humidity
- The availability of ventilation
- Foul smell in the housing area
- Loss in appetite
- Abnormal behavior
- Change in the reaction to humans
- Changes in the condition of the eyes such as cloudiness or discharge.
- Changes in the breathing patterns of the animals.

Cues from behavior
Healthy pigs are social and have normal interactions with their group. In diseased pigs, you will see the following changes in the animal itself and the group:

- The group will often reject the pig that is diseased. They may also become aggressive towards him.

- If more than one pig is unwell in the group, the diseased pigs tend to huddle.

- The pig does not show any interest in your or any other member of your family.

- The resting and lying patterns are very different from usual.

Cues from smell

Contrary to popular belief, pigs are not smelly and dirty creatures. In fact, when their living area or their bodies begin to emit a foul smell, it is an indication of some type of illness in the animal. Here are some changes in smell that you should be alert towards:

- The quality of the air in the living area seems poor.

- You will feel an excessive amount of moisture within the living area.

- The feces of the animal have a particularly foul odor.

- The animal emits a foul smell due to infections in the tissues.

- If you feel uncomfortable or sick when you enter the housing area of the pig, remember that the pigs experience the same. Make necessary changes to prevent disease and to control it from spreading.

Cues from touch

With your pet pigs, you are likely to spend a lot of time playing with them and also touching them. You will find some very obvious cues in the skin and in touch that you should be wary of:

- The limbs seem swollen.
- The temperature of the skin is higher or lower.
- The body has lumps and lesions that were not present before.

Once you have mastered all these cues, you will be able to understand when your pig requires medical attention. That being said, you also need to make sure that you have a good vet who is qualified to treat pigs. While your regular vets can help you with mild and common cases, in more severe cases you will need someone who specializes in treating farm animals such as pigs. The next section will tell you everything that you need to know about finding the perfect vet for your pig.

2. Finding the perfect vet

Pigs are usually listed as exotic animals, as not all vets are equipped to treat them. While you can take your pig to a regular vet for emergencies, you will need someone who is more qualified and one who has a better understanding of the anatomy of these animals.

Usually, a vet who has specialized in treating farm animals should be ideal for your Kunekune pig. You will need a specialized vet especially in case of major surgeries and treatments including neutering and spaying your pig.

There are some simple steps that you can use to tell if a vet is ideal for you or not. First you need to know what the right questions to ask are. Following that, you can examine the facility and get to know the personality of the vet to make sure that you feel comfortable taking your pet pig to him or her.

The questions that you should ask your vet

- What are the charges for each consultation and what do you include in each of them?

- Is it necessary for the pig to have a wellness check before any surgery? Does this come with an additional fee?

- Do you provide any discounts for rescue organizations?

- Have you worked with rescue pigs or breeders before? If the vet has worked with them, you can be assured that he or she has a lot of experience.

- How many Kunekune pigs have you neutered or spayed?

- In case of an emergency, do you have any after-hours facility?

- Are payments accepted online or over the phone?

- What is the preferred weight and age when it comes to spaying or neutering a pig? A pig that is 1 year old or over 60 pounds in weight should not be spayed or neutered. Your vet should be able to provide you with this basic information if he or she has any experience with treating pigs.

- What type of anesthesia is used in case of surgeries in pigs?

- Are there any facilities to provide care for the pig after surgery?

- Do you provide any home visits in case the pig cannot be brought to you? If so, what are the charges for the same?

- How do you perform hoof trims? Does the pig need a sedative or an anesthesia?

- Are you familiar with any other pigs that are kept as pets locally? If so, would the owner be able to provide a recommendation or a narration of their experience?

- How are the pigs restrained when you are examining them?

- In case you are dealing with an unfamiliar situation, do you know of any other experts that you can consult with?

- What is the typical waiting period for each appointment?

- Will you be able to provide a detailed vaccination schedule for my pig?

Some of these question are general and others are more specific. When you ask questions about procedures or certain illnesses with pigs, make sure that you know what the right answers to them are in order to be sure that your vet has enough experience and information.

Choosing the right vet

Being comfortable with the veterinarian that you choose is very important. Their approach towards treating pigs is an important factor in deciding whether you want to continue with a particular facility or not. After all, your vet is going to be a very vital part of your journey with your pig. Sometimes, you may have conflicting ideas when it comes to treating your animal.

For instance, some vets believe that pain killers or anesthesia are not necessary when it comes to pigs. However, they do feel pain and you may want more humane methods of providing pain free treatment to your pet.

In case your vet does not routinely provide any pain medication to pigs, you can always ask if he or she will do so upon request. It is very important that your vet respects your feelings towards your pet even if he or she does not follow a certain practice. If a vet refuses, then you always have the option of looking elsewhere.

Make sure that you ask many questions. The staff and the veterinarian should be willing to provide you with satisfactory answers. If your vet seems rushed and unwilling to take time to answer queries, it is also an indication that you need to look for other options.

Most often, the inability to answer questions is a sign of inexperience with a certain species of animal. This can be devastating if your vet is unable to recognize the crucial signs of a fatal condition. Even worse, the vet may make some irreparable errors when performing a surgery on your pig. If you are uncomfortable, do not settle with a certain vet. Make sure that you keep looking till you find one that you are fully satisfied with.

When it comes to anesthesia, it can be a very important indication of experience on the vet's part. The safest anesthesia to give to pigs is Isoflourane gas. In case your vet is using another type of anesthesia, make sure you ask him or her why they chose the latter. He should be willing to discuss the risks and the advantages of a certain type of anesthesia that he chooses.

Here is a quick summary of the factors that indicate that you need to find another vet for your pig:

- The vet does not give you enough time.
- The vet shows no compassion for your pet.
- The vet is unwilling to look for resources to accommodate your needs as a client.
- The vet does not seem to have enough information about treating pigs.

Where to look for a vet
You can look up the official website of any Kunekune pig association in your country to find several qualified vets. You also have the option of asking for recommendations from a veterinarian that you already know.

The internet is always a great option to find vets who are located at a convenient distance from you.

The location of the vet is very important, as he or she should be accessible in case of an emergency. The closer the facility, the better it is. Once you have short listed the clinics around you, make sure that you visit it once before you make any final decision. You must meet the vet in person to understand how comfortable he or she makes you feel. You can also fix an appointment for a routine check of your Kunekune pig. However, it is necessary to have options for veterinarians before you bring a pig home.

3. Vaccination schedule for Kunekune pigs
Vaccinations are the most important preventive measure that you can take with respect to Kunekune pigs. In some states, certain vaccinations are compulsory by law and you need to have enough documents to show that your pig has, indeed, received them all.

What are vaccinations?
A vaccine is loaded with antigens from disease causing bacteria, parasites or virus. These are given in mild doses in the form of an injection to trigger an immune response in the pig's body. This will help keep the pig protected in case there is any infection from these organisms in the future.

A vaccine can contain living organisms as well. These will multiply in the body of the pig to trigger the same response. Then, you also have the option of providing a vaccine with an inactive organism that is not going to multiply.

In the case of a live vaccine, the organism is stabilized and the virulence is reduced. This means that even with the organism multiplying in the body of the pig, no infection or disease will be caused. One example of this type of live vaccine is the classic swine fever vaccination.

Live vaccines have several advantages. To begin with, they are more potent because they actually multiply in the body. This provides immunity that lasts longer. However, when they are not stored properly or administered correctly, the organism may die, making the vaccine ineffective. You also need to make sure that the organisms are stable and will not cause any infection.

The most common type of inactive vaccine given to pigs is the Erysipelas Vaccine. There are eight steps to giving this vaccine to a pig:

- The bacteria are cultured in a broth.

- Then the bacteria are all killed.

- A type of liquid is added to this broth.

- The vaccine is produced once the two liquids mix together.

- A pre-decided number of bacteria are injected into the body of the pig.
- A second dose is given after 14 days of the first one to complete the immune response.

- After 7 days of the injection, the pig is fully protected.

You also have the option of antigen vaccines that are synthesized artificially. These are in the experimental phase still. It is possible to improve the immunity that inactive vaccines produce by adding certain substances like aluminum hydroxide. Some forms of oils can also be used.

In the case of any oily adjuvant, it is necessary to check for any local reactions that may be caused. This can also occur in the body of the human, when you are injecting it, for instance.

There may be some toxins even in vaccines that have been inactivated completely. They will create an immune response but will not be toxic to the animal. When toxins are modified, they are also known as toxoids.

The advantage with live vaccines is that the gene which is responsible for causing a certain disease is altogether removed. The response of the vaccine may vary from one animal to the other.

What are autogenous vaccines?
These vaccines are manufactured by bacteria that has been isolated from a pig that is already diseased. These types of vaccine can only be made with a license and can only be used on the farm that has obtained a license for it. Your vet will be able to help you create these vaccines.

These vaccines are usually suggested on farms with large groups of pigs where there could be a disease outbreak for which any standard vaccine is not available.

These vaccines are usually derived from bacteria such as:

- *E.coli*
- Salmonella

- Pasturella
- *Streptococcus sius*
- *Hawmophilys parasius*
- *Actinobacillus pleuropneumoniae*

The only issue with having a whole herd vaccinated is that blood tests cannot be used to detect a certain organism in case of a disease outbreak as most of the pigs will test positive to them. To prevent this, gene deleted vaccines have been created.

In these vaccines, a gene code that causes the disease is removed completely. That way, even when the organism does multiply in the body of the pig, disease is not caused.

There are several new generations of vaccines that are constantly being developed for pigs to help them stay healthier for longer.

Vaccination guidelines for pigs

When it comes to vaccinating your pig, the first thing that you need to do is have a word with your vet and make sure that you understand all the city ordinances. In different regions, the risk of certain diseases may be higher or lower.

In some cities, certain vaccinations are mandatory for pigs by law. In the case of pigs, a vaccination schedule as such is not possible. This is because the vaccination that they require may differ with each region and each situation of the individual pig owner.

For instance, in some cities it is mandatory to vaccinate your pig against rabies. However, there are no rabies vaccines for pigs that are approved. Having your pig vaccinated against rabies only means that the chances of contracting the disease are reduced. However, it does not mean that your pig is completely immune to the condition.

If you have a pet pig, chances are that he may not interact with any wild pigs or swine. However, it is mandatory to have him vaccinated against diseases that he may contract from other pigs.

Most of the vaccines available today are directed towards pigs that are raised in farm conditions, which are quite different to the conditions that we raise our pigs in. However, pet pigs are just as susceptible as commercial pigs when it comes to diseases that pigs commonly contract. These infections can be carried from one animal to the other and can also be spread through the soil or can be carried in the air. These factors are out of our control. Therefore, having your pig vaccinated is very important.

In the case of pigs, vaccinations depend on the following factors:

- Chances of exposure to a certain disease.
- The region that you live in.
- The environment that the pig is raised in.
- Veterinarian preferences.
- Laws in your city or state.

Here is an example of how these factors affect the vaccination schedule. Only 50% of vets will recommend having your pig vaccinated against rabies. However, if your pig does bite a person and is not vaccinated against rabies, it is legal in most states to take the pig away. Have him or her euthanized in order to check for any chances of rabies. Even off label vaccines can be used as long as the pig is vaccinated.

Now, vaccination schedule can also change based on the purpose that your pig us raised for. Here are a few examples:

Vaccination schedule for pet pigs and show pigs
Typically, the vaccination schedule for pigs will begin just after a week of them being born. Piglets should be vaccinated against mycoplasma, rhinitis, erysipelas and pneumonia.

Rhinitis is a disease that affects the tissues inside the nose of the animal. This is quite common in pigs. This disease is progressive and can release several toxins that eventually distort the nose of the animal.

Erusipelas is a type of skin disease that is caused by bacteria. Although it is not very common it can be deadly, which is why vaccinating your pig is necessary. This is true for pneumonia and mycoplasma as well.

Continuing the vaccination schedule
When the piglets are about 3 weeks old, it is necessary to vaccinate them against circovirus. This is a very common virus that affects pigs and can cause fatal diseases.

When the piglets are 4 weeks old, a booster shot for rhinitis as well as erysipelas should be provided. They must also be vaccinated against actinobacillus and pneumonia.

When the piglets are 8 weeks old, they should be vaccinated against any disease that can be caused by parasites. This includes polyserositis and

Glasser's disease. This will also keep the pig protected against Actinobacillus pleuropneumonia as well.

Important vaccinations for pigs

Here is a list of vaccines that are most recommended for pigs. Although the regulations may vary from state to state, it is a good idea to have your pig vaccinated against the following diseases just to be sure:

Erysipelas

- This is a very painful condition that can also be fatal at times. It can cause high fever in the animal and can impair the functioning of the blood vessels. Bruising and bleeding of the skin is also common.

- This condition can be carried by birds and the bacteria that causes is can be potent in soil for a long time.

- Most pigs will be exposed to this condition and it is best to have them vaccinated.

- The first shot should be provided when the pigs are 8 weeks old. A booster is provided 2 weeks after.

- The pigs should be vaccinated every year after this.

Tetanus

- This is another condition that is transmitted by bacteria in the soil. If you have an area shared by horses and pigs, especially, this vaccine is very important.

- Although pigs are resistant to tetanus infection, once they contract it, the condition is usually fatal.
- Pigs tend to roll around in dirt and mud. During this time, even the smallest cut can get infected.

- At the age of 8 weeks, pigs must be vaccinated for tetanus. A booster is given two weeks after.

- Following this, the pigs should be vaccinated every 6 months.

Leptospirosis

- This condition is caused by different kinds of bacteria. These bacteria are called serotypes and are related to one another.

- Pigs are vaccinated for serotypes that are most deadly and dangerous.

- This vaccine does not cover all the serotypes but does offer some partial immunity against most.

- This condition is carried by wild birds and animals and is often deposited in water bodies that the pigs could come in touch with. Raccoons are the most common carriers of the condition.

- This is also contagious to humans and is often carried in the urine of pigs. Making sure that you wash your hands every time you interact with your pig can prevent the condition from being transmitted.

- When they are 8 weeks old, piglets should be vaccinated for this condition. A booster is provided after two weeks.

- Following this, boosters are given every year.

Actinobacillus pleuropneumoniae

- This vaccine is given to pigs as a combination vaccine.

- When infected with this bacterium, pigs can succumb to severe respiratory diseases. It can also lead to permanent lung damage in case the animal does survive.

- This condition is less common in pet pigs.

- However, if you are breeding your pigs, make sure that he is vaccinated to keep the offspring immune.

- Most vaccines given to pigs include actinobacillus.

Rabies

- As discussed before, there is no vaccine for pigs that is licensed. Most often horse or dog vaccines are given to pigs. These vaccines also help the pig develop the necessary protective antibodies.

- Usually commercial pigs are never vaccinated for rabies.

- With pet pigs, it can become an issue if your pig bites someone. As per the law, a doctor is required to report any unvaccinated animal to the health department if he is not vaccinated.

- This could lead to quarantining the pig for up to 60 days. They can also be euthanized to test them for rabies.

- If the pig is vaccinated, he will only have to be quarantined in your home.

- Vaccination for pigs should be provided when the pig is 4 months old. Then, you need to provide a booster within a year. Following this, a booster should be provided every three years.

How effective are vaccines?

This depends quite a bit on the type of vaccine that is given. Generally, the vaccines given against intestinal and respiratory conditions are not as effective as the ones that are given against any systemic disease or a generalized disease.

There is only one exception to this rule, which is the vaccine for enzootic pneumonia. This is because immunity in this disease is cell mediated. If the vaccine is fed into the upper tract of the respiratory system, strong immunity is provided.

Vaccines can be ineffective sometimes, especially on farms, for the following reasons:

- The vaccine has some contamination.

- The vaccine failed to produce the level of immunity expected.

- The disease was already being incubated in the body of the pig when he was vaccinated.

- The vaccine was not stored correctly. Excessive heat usually renders a vaccine ineffective.

- The vaccine had been exposed to sunlight.

- The vaccination was past the date of expiry.

- The syringe or needle was faulty.

- The vaccine was destroyed by chemical sterilization.

- The presence of maternal antibody made the response of the vaccine poor.

- The injection technique used was faulty because of which the vaccine was injected and deposited in the fat, making it impossible for the body to absorb.

Handling vaccines

If you are stocking vaccines for your pig or have bought any vaccination to give to your pig yourself, then you need to make sure that they are handled well. Without proper management, vaccines are usually rendered ineffective. This means that your pet is not protected from the possible infections.

Here are some tips to handle vaccines correctly:

- Make sure you check the date of expiry.

- Store the vaccines in a fridge.

- Check the temperature of the vaccine every day. If they are frozen, vaccines are rendered useless.

- Make sure you follow the instructions.

- Do not store vaccines in the same fridge that you store meat in.
- Make sure you use a fresh needle for every pig.

- Vaccines and medicines should never be mixed.

- Needles must always be disposed using a sharps box.

- The syringe should be cleaned immediately after use if it is reusable.

- The bottle tops should always be cleaned before using.

- Make sure that you only use vaccines that are licensed in your country.

Follow a strict vaccination program for your pet pig to keep him safe and to also be responsible towards other possible pig farms and pets in your locality. In order to make sure that your pigs are all vaccinated correctly, you should also be familiar with the diseases that commonly affect pigs. The next chapter discusses each condition in detail to help you not only learn about them but also make sure that you are able to detect the signs and symptoms of these conditions early for easy treatment.

4. Common illnesses in Kunekune pigs
Like all breeds of animals, pigs are more susceptible to certain conditions. This chapter tells you about the symptoms, causes and possible treatments of the conditions that commonly affect the pigs.

Keeping yourself updated about diseases that are common in pigs will help you identify the symptoms easily. The first step towards a successful treatment program is to provide timely assistance to your pet. While pigs are generally hardy, most infections are severe, so it is possible that your pig will become seriously ill in a very short period of time if you are unable to detect early symptoms.

Diseases of the gastrointestinal system
These diseases are common among pigs because they tend to ingest several organisms through the soil when they are grazing. One of the most effective ways of prevention is to keep the pig indoors. Since they are opportunistic eaters, they are forever foraging for food, which requires you to restrict the diet and make sure that your pig gets only certain portions of food that include grass along with other low calorie foods.

Ingestion of foreign objects
Sometimes, pigs may ingest small foreign objects while foraging. This will pass through the GI tract without any issue in most cases. In some cases, it may cause very mild gastritis that only needs antibiotic therapy.

When the pig ingests any large object, chances are that it may go into the small intestine and cause several health issues. You must watch out for the symptoms of possible foreign body ingestion.

Symptoms:

- Colic pain
- Vomiting
- Dehydration
- Anorexia
- Scanty production of feces
- Bloating of the abdominal region.

Treatment:

- A radiograph is needed to check for the foreign object in the GI of the pig.

- In most cases, surgical correction is necessary.

- If it is not lodged inside too deeply, fluids can be used to flush it out, followed by antibacterial therapy.

Colibacillosis

This condition is caused by *E.Coli* bacteria. It mostly affects younger pigs. It leads to a high mortality rate if the piglets do not get good quality colostrum within 24 hours of being born. Mostly, older pigs are immune to this condition.

Symptoms:

- Frequent diarrhea
- Dehydration
- Acidosis.

Preventive care:

Since this condition does not have any visible symptoms, it is necessary to take the following measures to prevent infection altogether:

- Provide good sanitation to prevent the bacteria from multiplying in the environment of the pig.

- Provide necessary vaccination to the sow.

Treatment:

- Injectable or oral gentamicin
- Injectable ceftiofur.

Enterocolitis

This is a condition that is caused by *Salmonella typhimurium*. Pigs can be infected at any age. However, it is more common in piglets that have just been weaned. When pigs are exposed to garbage cans, other pigs, fecal matter of animals of other species, they can get infected.

Symptoms:

- Abnormal feces
- Mild to severe feces
- Blood in the feces
- Mucus in the feces.
- Distended abdomen
- Rectal prolapse.

Preventive care:

Providing necessary vaccination can help prevent this condition.

Treatment:

- The condition is diagnosed with fecal cultures and a study of the history of a group of pigs.

- In case of rectal prolapse, surgical correction is possible.

- 2.2mg of gentamicin for three days can help in curing the condition if detected early.

Septicemia

After weaning, piglets are susceptible to infections by *S.Choleraesuis* causing septicemia or bacteremia. These bacteria are transmitted through the same sources as Salmonella.

Symptoms:

- Mild to severe diarrhea
- Anorexia
- Fever
- Lethargy
- Blueness in extremities
- Death.

Treatment:

The treatment is similar to *Salmonella typhimurium* infections. However, since this condition can affect people with low immunity, it is a bigger threat.

Constipation

This is a very common problem seen in pigs. It is necessary to make sure that your pig has been examined carefully before you provide any treatment for this condition. Normally, low water intake is a cause of constipation, but it could also be a symptom of another form of infection.

Symptoms:

- The fecal matter is in the form of multiple balls instead of single cylindrical formations.

Treatment:

- The pig is usually treated with a mild laxative that is given with the food.

- It is very important to make sure that the medication is not forcefully fed to the animal, as it can lead to death or pneumonia, especially when give with mineral oil.
- Make sure that your pig drinks a lot of water. Adding some fruit juice can improve water intake.

- The pig must get regular exercise to alleviate the condition.

Rectal prolapse

This normally occurs when there is some irritation in bowel movement or when the pig strains to pass feces. It can also be the result of Salmonella infection. There are several other causal factors such as:

- Persistent cough
- Genetic predisposition
- Cystitis
- Urolithiasis
- Previous repair of rectal prolapse.

Symptoms:

- Blood in stool
- Swollen abdomen
- Constipation
- Protruding rectum.

Treatment:

- In mild cases, a simple procedure that requires a purse-string closure of the rectal area is possible.

- In more complicated cases, excision with surgery is needed. However, this can result in a prolapse.

Intestinal Carcinoma

This is mostly seen in older pigs and there is no cure for the condition. In fact, it can only be confirmed after a post mortem report.

Symptoms:

- Vomiting
- Anemia
- Melena
- Chronic weigh loss.

This ultimately results in the death of the animal.

Skin diseases in Kunkune pigs

The skin of pigs, in general, is prone to a lot of infections. This is mostly because of the structure of their bodies and also the fact that they tend to wallow in mud in order to keep themselves cool. Here are some common skin diseases in Kunekune pigs:

Dry and flaky skin

This is a condition that is normally seen in Kunekune pigs at some point in their lives. It can vary from mild to severe.

Treatment:

- Wipe the skin down with clean, wet towels every week.

- You can use aloe vera gel or special moisturizing creams to reduce dryness.

- Supplementing the diet with fatty acids provides long-term relief from the condition. However, make sure you only give the pig the right amount to prevent the chances of obesity.

Sarcoptic mange

This is one of the most common parasitic diseases in pigs. This condition can also affect humans and in most cases, owners of pigs with this skin disease tend to have itchy skin on the abdomen and the arms. It is caused by mites and is common in younger pigs that normally get the infection from the mother. In case of older pigs, they tend to get this from other pigs in their group.

Symptoms:

- Extreme itchiness of the skin
- Red patches and rashes all over the skin.

Treatment:
- The infected pigs must be isolated from the group.

- Medicines such as ivermectin and doramectin can be given for 2-3 weeks.

- For pigs that are younger, preventive injections should be given along with parasiticides.

Melanoma

This is a type of skin tumor that is very common in pigs.

Symptoms:

- Lumps on the surface of the skin
- Hair depigmentation
- Depigmentation of the iris
- Paleness and depigmentation of the skin.

Treatment:

- Removal of the tumor
- Examination of the tumor to check if the condition may recur.

Sunburn

Even though Kunekune pigs have hair on the surface of their skin, they tend to get severe sunburn. This usually occurs when they are exposed to sunlight that is high in intensity. Sudden exposure to harsh sunlight can also cause the condition.

Symptoms:

- Lesions on the skin
- Weakness of the hind limb
- Pain in the hind limb
- Vocalization of the pain when walking or even standing.

Treatment:

- Treatment is based on the symptoms.

- It is necessary to avoid any exposure to sunlight in the future

Bleeding back syndrome

Also known as dippity pig syndrome, this condition affects pigs commonly but the causal factor still remains unknown. The symptoms are very similar to sunburn but the pigs have no history of sun exposure.

Symptoms:

- Vocalization of pain
- Circular shaped lesions that ooze serum
- The lesions are mostly seen on the lumbar surfaces.

Treatment:

- Activity in the affected pigs should be restricted
- Symptomatic treatment is provided.
- The condition may recur.

Erysipelas

This is a bacterial condition that is caused by *Erysipelothrix rhusiopathiae*. This bacterium is commonly seen in the tonsil tissue of pigs. It can affect both young pigs and ones that are growing.

The organism can be shed by pigs that carry them through the feces or through the secretions of the nose and the eyes, causing infection in the other pigs. The outbreak of the disease can range from normal to chronic.

Acute symptoms:

- High fever
- Painful joints
- Skin lesions
- Blueness of the skin
- Rhomboid lesions
- Sudden death.

Chronic symptoms:

- Enlarged joints
- Lameness
- Valvular lesions

- Heavy breathing
- Lethargy.

Treatment:

- The bacteria are sensitive to penicillin.

- The affected pig can be given penicillin shots at 12-hour intervals.

- Tetracyclins can also be given to the pig.

- Symptoms of fever can be treated with aspirin mixed in the water.

Prevention:

- Vaccinating your pig against erysipelas is a must.

- Not giving your pig annual booster shots can lead to outbreaks of the condition.

- Live vaccines and bacterins can be given to the pigs via water.

Musculoskeletal diseases of Kunekune pigs

Diseases that affect the musculoskeletal system tend to make the pigs immobile and less active. This can lead to various other health issues. Therefore, the earlier they are treated the better. Here are the common musculoskeletal diseases that affect pigs.

Lameness

Because of the structure of their body, pigs are very susceptible to ligament damage and muscle pulls. They also tend to have fractures in their limbs quite often.

Fractures are normally the result of some trauma such as dog bites, restraint, kicks from other farm animals or accidents like falling from tall furniture.

Symptoms:

- Inability to walk

- Vocalization of the pain
- Compromised posture
- Limping
- Fractures in the femur, elbow or distal humerus.

Treatment:

- The recovery of lameness is quite rapid if the pig is kept under constant observation.

- Injury to any limb or to the back of the animal is treated with anti-inflammatory medicines such as flunixin meglumine, aspirin and glucocorticoids.

- In case of fractures, the joint is immobilized with a cast.

- Screws or plates may be necessary in case of some fractures.

Infectious arthritis

This condition is normally observed in older pigs. It can be caused by several strains of bacteria including *Steptococcus spp, Erysipelothrix rhusiopathiae, M.hyohinis, Mycoplasma hyosynoviae. Haemophilus parasuis and Staphylococcus spp.*

Symptoms:

- Lameness without any visible swelling in the joints
- Lameness in multiple limbs
- Vocalization of the pain.

Treatment:
- Antimicorbial medicines such as lincomycin for 3 days.

- Anti-inflammatory medicines to manage the pain.

In some cases, these symptoms could also be indicative of polyarthritis which is seen in the younger pigs. They get this disease from the mother.

Degenerative arthritis or any chronic inflammation of the joints due to polyarthritis usually leads to euthanasia. These symptoms are also seen in the case of osteochondritis. However, in this condition the hip, shoulder and elbow are commonly affected. In case of smaller pigs like the Kunekune pig, this condition is not very common.

Overgrown hooves or cracked hooves

This is a very common cause of lameness in pigs. It is important for your pig to have ample exercise and also areas with abrasive surfaces to walk on. This helps keep the hooves trimmed.

Prevention:

Routine trimming of the hooves is the best way to prevent elongation, cracks and overgrowth of the hooves. This has to be done under sedation or with some anesthesia.

Treatment:

- Cleaning of the cracked hoof is recommended.

- Antiseptics such as iodine can be used to clean the hooves.

- Antimicrobial therapy with ampicillin or ceftiofur is recommended to reduce pain and inflammation.

Zygomucosis

This condition is caused by bacteria called *Mucor spp.*

Symptoms:

- The symptoms of this condition commonly occur in the distal hind limb.

- Growth of infected tissue on the foot is observed.

- Abscesses may be present on the food as well.

Treatment:
In chronic conditions, amputation is the only remedy to prevent the condition from spreading. Preventive care such as good sanitation is a must.

Tetanus

This condition is caused when wounds are contaminated. The common reasons for these wounds are skin abrasions, dog bites, surgical procedures and abrasions of the oral cavity. It is caused by a strain of bacteria called the *Closrtridium tetani.*

Symptoms:

- Fits
- Hypersensitivity
- Stiffness in muscles and joints
- Erect tail
- Spasms in the muscles of the face and the ears
- High rate of mortality.

Prevention:

- Tetanus toxoid vaccine should be given to the pigs routinely.

- IM should be administered to any pig that is recovering from a surgery.

Treatment:

- The pig should be given large doses of tetanus antitoxin.

- Penicillin can be used in the early stages of infection.

- Supportive therapy is recommended to help improve mobility in the animal that is recovering.

Diseases of the nervous system

Lack of coordination in the limbs and constant spasms are common in the case of any nervous system-related diseases in pigs. They can be caused by several factors including infection and improper care. Here are some nervous system diseases that affect pigs.

Systemic bacterial infection

This condition is normally caused by strains of bacteria including *Salmonella choleraisuis, Streptocuccus spp, Streptococcus suis type*

2,*Haemophilus parasuis* and *E.coli*. This infection can also be caused by some strains of gram-negative bacteria.

Symptoms:

- Abnormality in the posture
- Head tilting
- Circling
- Seizures
- Lack of coordination
- Staggering
- Depression
- Fever
- High rate of mortality.

Treatment:

- Antibacterial therapy with medicines such as florfenicol in the early stages is very effective.

- Usually treatment is ineffective in case of this condition.

If the infection is caused by *S.sius Type 2* it is necessary for you to visit the doctor as it is a zootonic condition that affects humans as well.

Overheating

Taking enough care to provide shade and other options to cool the body off during summers is very important for pigs. Overheating can lead to several symptoms that indicate that the nervous system is affected.

Symptoms:

- Slow breathing with the mouth open
- Inactivity
- Depression
- Fever that is fluctuating.

Treatment:
- The animal may respond to simple treatment techniques such as a cooler resting space.

- Ice bags on the head.

- Cooling the head with water.

- Cold water enemas.

- Packing the body with ice in case of extreme conditions is highly recommended.

Salt toxicity

This is a condition that is caused when the animal is deprived of water for more than 36 hours. When sudden rehydration is provided, symptoms of salt toxicity are noticed. It can also be caused by a diet that is high in salty foods.

Symptoms:

- Walking aimlessly
- Postural abnormality
- Blindness
- Seizures.

Treatment:

- Gradually rehydrating the animal.

- Symptomatic treatment.

In most cases, the pigs can be stabilized when they are fully blind or have become paralyzed. This is true especially in cases of brain tissue damage.

Seizures

This condition normally affects pigs that are over 1 year of age. They may have between 1-2 seizures each month to multiple seizures in a single day. If the seizures are not frequent, medication is not necessary.

Treatment:
- In the case of frequent seizures, diazepam is provided:

- When the condition is chronic, phenobarbital is recommended for effective treatment.

Diseases of the respiratory system

The diseases of respiratory system lead to breathing difficulties. This makes them less active and also leads to several health issues eventually.

Atrophic rhinitis

This is a condition that is caused by at least two different organisms. It may also have several casual agents that are non-infectious such as high levels of ammonia and dust. One of the most common causal factors is *Bordetella bronchiseptica.*

Pigs normally get infected by rodents, cats, dogs and other animals that may harbor the microorganism.

Symptoms:

- Sneezing
- Coughing
- Inflammation of tear ducts
- Tear stains
- Shortening of the upper jaw
- Distortion of the jaws
- Lesions in the oral cavity
- Softening of the nasal cavity.

Prevention:

Preventive care is the only option with this condition. The options to prevent the condition are:

- Better ventilation in the living area.

- Better hygiene.

- Dust free feed.

- Quarantining when new pigs are introduced to the herd.

- Vaccination programs for newborn pigs.

Treatment:

Although they are not very effective, some medicines that can be tried include tetracyclins, ceftiofur and sulfonamides.

Pneumonia

This condition is very serious in Kunekune pigs, as they already have a rather short lung capacity. It is usually caused by an infection from *Mycoplasma hypopneumoniae*. This compromises the immunity of the lungs and eventually leads to infection by a strain of bacteria called *Pasturella multocidia*.

In younger pigs, they may contract this from the mother, but in most cases this infection occurs when pigs mix with other infected animals.

This condition may also result from sudden weather changes or any other form of stress.

Symptoms:

- Coughing
- Stunted growth
- Difficulty in breathing
- Lesions on the lungs
- Blue or purple colored lungs.

Prevention:

- Hygienic living conditions.

- Ethical husbandry practices.

- Isolation of affected pigs.

- Proper ventilation of the living area.

- Avoiding any form of overcrowding in the pen.

- Vaccination against the condition.

Treatment:

- Antibiotics are administered in case of these infections

Pleuropneumonia

This condition in pigs is almost always life threatening. It is the result of an infection by *Actinobacillus pleuropneumoniae.* Pigs may develop infections due to exposure to other infected animals or from the mother.

Symptoms:

- Fever
- Cough
- Lung tissue damage
- Lethargy
- Difficulty in breathing
- Sudden death.

Prevention:

- Vaccination against pleuoropneumoniae.

- Proper husbandry practices.

- Good ventilation.

- Isolation of an infected animal.

Treatment:

- Treatment is only possible when the condition is detected in the early stages.

- Penicillin and ceftiofur are effective antibiotics against this condition.

Swine Influenza

This is a viral condition that is normally seen in pigs that tend to come in contact with pigs from other farms or homes. This includes pigs that are taken to petting zoos or exhibitions. The condition tends to subside on its own after 7-10 days but can also be fatal in the case of a severe infection.

Swine flu is caused by the Swine Influenza Virus or SIV. This is a type of virus that belongs to the Influenza A group. These viruses contain a hemagglutinating antigen and a neuraminidase antigen that are represented as H1N1, H1N2 and H1N3 depending upon the subtype of virus that is responsible for the condition.

Symptoms:

- Coughing
- Anorexia
- Excessive thirst
- Discharge in the mucous membrane
- Discharge from the eyes
- Weakness
- Prostration
- Sudden death
- Lesions in the thoracic cavity.

Prevention:

- Vaccination is the only option to prevent this condition in pigs.

- Good management practices.

- No overcrowding of the living area.

- Preventing exposure to dust.

Treatment:

- Administering expectorants.

- Antimicrobials in case of any secondary infection due to bacteria.

Diseases of the Urinary System

In case your pig is struggling to urinate, it could be due to some infection in the urinary system. When pigs are kept in unhygienic conditions, these infections are quite common and can affect the pig.

Cystitis and uriothiasis

If you have more than one pig at home, these conditions should be watched out for. They may eventually lead to kidney failure if left untreated. The condition is caused by a type of bacteria called *Actinobaculum sius.* These organisms are very difficult to eradicate.

This condition is responsible for several deaths in sows, especially the dry ones. Usually sows do not respond to any treatment and may die suddenly.

Symptoms:

- Ill appearance
- Lack of appetite
- Weight loss
- Red membrane in the eyes
- Blood or pus in the vulva
- Wetness in region around the vulva
- Abortion in case of pregnant sows
- Obvious pain and discomfort
- Grinding of teeth.

Symptoms when cystitis occurs alone:

- The disease seems prolonged but is usually not fatal
- Pus in the urine
- Discharge in the vulva
- Inflammation of the vagina.

Treatment:

- Antibiotic treatment.

- Administration of lincomycin.

- Injecting a weaning sow with penicillin or amoxicillin.

- Supplement administration after 21 days of mating.

- Antibiotic liquids in the food or water.

Chronic kidney failure

This condition almost always affects the older pigs. It can lead to improper urination and even inability to concentrate the urine. In older pigs, it eventually leads to death.

Symptoms:

- Anorexia
- Dehydration
- Lethargy
- Azotemia
- Ammonia odor in the breath
- Low body temperature.

Treatment:

- Antibiotic treatment with procaine penicillin.

- Rehydration.

5. First aid for Kunekune pigs

For every pet owner, being prepared for an emergency is extremely important. You need to know what to do if your pig begins to vomit, sustains injuries, chokes or has any other type of health issue.

The biggest mistake that pet owners make is to check for solutions online. The first call that you make should be to your vet in case of any emergency. Make sure that you have his or her number readily available. If your pig is being taken care of while you are away, the caretaker should have this number as well.

Signs that your pig needs first aid

- The pig refuses to eat or drink.

- The pig becomes unresponsive.

- The pig begins to shake violently or becomes still.
- The pig presses the head against the wall.

- The pig starts to move around in circles.

- The pig is gasping for air.

- The pig begins to vomit blood or has bloody diarrhea.

- The temperature of the body is below 98 degrees or is above 103 degrees.

- The pig has a sign of an obvious fracture.

- The pig strains to urinate or defecate.

- A pregnant pig is unable to deliver the piglet even after 1 hour of pushing.

- The pig has a weak pulse or a very rapid pulse.

- The pig is bleeding.

- The pig seems to have a heat stroke.

- The pig becomes unconscious.

Basic first aid

Here are some basic first aid techniques that you should become aware of when you bring a pig home

Choking

One of more of the following symptoms indicate that your pig is choking on some foreign object or a piece of food:

- Excessive drooling
- Gagging
- Excessive coughing
- Whistling sound while breathing
- Blue gums, nose, ears or tongue
- Loss of consciousness
- Inability to vocalize
- Strained breathing.

First aid for choking

- If the pig is conscious and allows you to put your finger into the mouth, then use your finger to reach in and sweep the object out.

- In the case of a string, make sure you pull it out very gently.

- If the pig is unconscious, you can try the finger sweep.

- Pigs have a smooth, bony structure deep in their throat. You need to make sure that you do not attempt to pull at it during the finger sweep.

- If you feel the object but are unable to pull it out, try to push it in deeper to open the airway and then rush your pet to the pig.

- Extending the neck and the head is also an easy way to open the airway.

- A sharp slap on the chest wall is also used to clear the airway.

If the pig is still not breathing

In case your pig is still not breathing, the Heimlich maneuver or rescue breathing will help. Here are some tips to perform this on your pig.

The Heimlich maneuver
- Lay the pig down on one side.

- Place your hand on the back and another hand on his belly, just below the ribs.

- Push the belly in and up several times.

- Then perform the finger sweep to check if the object is out.

- If this does not work, place both your hands on the chest and then thrust them downwards.

Rescue breathing
- When the pig becomes unconscious or is evidently struggling to breathe, rescue breathing is useful.

- Cover the nose of the pig with your mouth and then blow into it forcefully.

- In piglets, the mouth should be held shut when doing this.

- In larger pigs, you must also cup the muzzle with the hands while you force the air in.

- A sign that this technique is working is that the lungs begin to expand.

- When the lungs have expanded fully, you can stop and then wait for the chest to contract again.

- Repeat this rescue breathing technique at least 3 times.

- If the pig does not show signs of breathing, you must continue this every 25 minutes in case of adult pigs and every 20 minutes in case of older pigs.

- If the pig is unconscious, this should be repeated every 10-15 minutes.

- Make sure your pig is on the way to the veterinary facility when you begin rescue breathing.

CPR and rescue breathing should be continued until the pig can get some veterinary attention.

Wounds
Pigs may sustain several types of injuries. The most common wounds in case of pigs are:

- Abrasions
- Lacerations
- Punctures
- Burns.

When should you take your pet to the vet?

- If the injury has caused a significant amount of trauma with chances of injury to ligaments, bones and muscles.
- There is a need for stitches or sutures.

- You are unable to control the bleeding.

- The pig needs to be sedated.

- You are unable to clean the wound properly.

Cleaning the wound:

Flush the injured area with some tap water. If it is superficial, you can scrub it gently to remove any debris. If it is deep, do not attempt to scrub. In the case of a bite, use saline or any other antibacterial wash to clean the wound. Using 3% hydrogen peroxide is recommended. Make sure you apply some pressure on the affected area when you are washing the wound. It should be clean and should have some sheen on the surface.

Managing severe wounds

- If the wound is severe, rush the pet to the vet immediately.

- The wound should be cleaned and dressed while you are on your way to the vet.

- In the case of severe bleeding, make sure that you apply pressure on the area.

- Gather details about the injury.

- Any wounds that are over 6 hours old cannot be stitched.

Dressing a wound

- Apply a recommended topical antibiotic.

- This can be used only within 48 hours of the injury. If not, even the probiotics that work on healing the wound will be killed.

- Keep the wound moist until you get the pet to the doctor.

- You can use wound honey to do this.

Checking the wound for infection
- If your pet develops a fever or if there is any evident swelling in the area, it is a sign of infection.

- The wound is warm to the touch.

- The skin around the wound seems to be irritated and red.

- Infections should be attended to immediately as they can cause severe damage to the internal tissues, bones and even the organs of the animal when they become septic.

Shock

In medical terms, shock occurs when the body does not have enough supply of oxygen or when the tissues are unable to use oxygen properly. Shock can be life threatening and is usually the result of a serious injury. You need to give your pig adequate care including IV fluids in extreme cases. Any treatment for shock is only effective when it is prompt.

What is shock?

- The cardiovascular system pumps blood through blood vessels to different parts of the body.

- The blood fills the system to capacity and carries oxygen and other substances like nutrients to different parts of the body.

- It also helps remove any waste from the cells.

- If the system fails to deliver a required amount of this fluid, it can lead to an accumulation of toxins and also reduced levels of oxygen.

- When this deprivation of oxygen becomes extreme, some tissues of the heart may die and cannot be restored.

Symptoms of shock

- The pig is either too excited or too subdued.

- The heart rate becomes rapid.

- Gums become pale.
- The pulse is more pronounced.

- Respiration is shallow, rapid or deep.

- The body of the pig feels cold to the touch.

- Rectal temperature is low.

- Eyes look glazed.

- The mental condition of the animal begins to deteriorate

How to treat shock

- Help the pig breathe with rescue breathing or CPR.

- If he is bleeding, apply pressure on the wound.

- Immobilize him gently.

- If he seems too aggressive, you may have to keep him in a crate.

- Cover the body with blankets to prevent heat loss.

- Stabilize fractures, if any.

- Rush your pet to the vet.

What you should not do

- Never give the pig any water or medication through the mouth.

- Never make him walk or move.

- Observe the condition and make sure you ask for veterinary help.

Water deprivation or salt toxicity
There are several reasons why pigs may be deprived of water. In the case of dehydration, excessive salt in the body can lead to serious issues.

What to do if the pig is not drinking water

- Try bottled water or filtration pitchers.

- Add some juice such as pineapple or grape juice to the water. These fruit juices are also acidic in nature, offering several health benefits when added in small quantities.

- Add some food to the water. However, make sure that you keep a check on your pig's calorie consumption.

- Give him fruits and vegetables that have high water content.

- During the hotter months, you can give him frozen vegetables.

- Make sure that the water bowl is not dry. If the water is dirty or smelly, pigs tend to overturn the bowl.

- If you are feeding pellets to your pig, you can also try soaking them to improve hydration.

- Increase the size of the bowl if you notice that it is always empty.

- Add some concrete to the underside of the water bowl to make sure that the pig cannot tip it over.

What is salt poisoning?

The salt regulation system in pigs is quite poor, making it even more important for them to have enough water intake. Salt poisoning is usually seen in pigs when they consume more water than necessary. This leads to swelling in the brain and can even be fatal.

Salt poisoning in pigs is of two kinds:

- **Through the diet:** If the food is rich in salts, then pigs tend to have an increased amount of sodium in their body. Make sure you do not give them too many salty treats, which also make them thirstier, leading to excessive water consumption.

- **Through dehydration:** If water become available to a pig after a spell of dehydration, he will drink too much of it, leading to salt toxicity.

Symptoms of salt poisoning
- Tremors
- Reduced appetite
- Increased level of thirst
- Fever
- Tremors
- Lack of coordination in the body

- Diarrhea
- Fever
- Coma
- Seizure
- Sudden death.

What you should do

- Remove all the water sources.

- Call your vet immediately.

- If your pig is dehydrated, make sure you give him water in small amounts until he loses interest in it.

Fractures

Any crack or break in the bone is referred to as a fracture. The first aid that you give to your pig depends upon the type of fracture. The pig may sustain a fracture when he jumps off tall furniture, falls on a slippery floor or in the case of an attack.

The types of fractures in pigs are:

- Closed fracture where there is no sign of any wound.

- Open fracture where the pig also has open wounds.

- Dislocation where the bone is displaced from a joint.

- Sprain where the ligament or tendon in a particular region is affected.

- Tears in the ligaments.

What you should do
- Make sure that the pig is contained in order to prevent any chances of bites or attacks.

- If there is a wound, apply direct pressure to it.

- In case of an open fracture, cover the affected area with gauze.

- In case of fractures in the limbs, use a towel under the abdomen as a sling to support the fractured bone.

- Take your pet to the vet immediately.

What you should not do

- Never flush a wound in the case of an open fracture, as it may lead to further contamination.

- Never provide any over the counter painkillers.

- In the case of a protruding bone, never attempt to push it back into place.

Fever

There are several causes of fever in pigs including infections, toxicity, inflammation or trauma. The normal temperature of the pig's body is between 98 and 101 degree F. If the temperature exceeds 104, make sure you take your pig to the vet immediately.

What you should do

- Give the pig more fluids. Try mixing apple or cranberry juice with water.

- Give him a Popsicle or an ice cube.

- Wrap ice in a towel and place it in the pig's resting area.

- Use a cool cloth on the abdomen, neck and head.

- Moisten the hair of your pig with cool water.

- Direct a fan towards his body.

- Never give your pig any aspirin. You can give him Tylenol used for children. You can give him a dose of 5mg per pound of his body weight. If the fever does not subside in three days, see the vet immediately.

Additional first aid tips

Here are some additional tips to make sure that your pig gets the necessary attention at the right time. In many cases, this can be a life saver:

- To know if your pig is dehydrated, pull the skin in between his shoulder blades. If it remains tented and does not bounce back into place when you let go, it means that the pig is dehydrated.

- Pet poisoning can lead to dilated pupils, foaming at the mouth, excessive drooling or external and internal bleeding.

- Heat stroke leads to increased body temperature, sudden collapse, panting, increased heart rate and salivation. Make sure that the pig is submerged in cold water immediately.

First aid kit for pigs
Having a first aid kit in place can help you give your pig better attention in case of an emergency. Here are some things that you should include in your first aid kit for pigs:

- Koolaid in any flavor to increase blood sugar or to help the pig drink water. It can also be used to give the pig certain medicines.

- Pedialyte to restore the electrolytes in the body in case of severe diarrhea or vomiting.

- Heating pad in case the pig loses body heat and also to keep him warm when the temperatures drop.

- Digital thermometer.

- Different sized syringes to administer fluids to the pig.

- Ice packs for injuries and to cool the body down.

- Q-tips to apply ointments.

- KY Jelly to moisten the skin in case of any injury.

- Gauze and other bandaging material.

- Styptic powder for bleeding hooves.

- Epsom salt to relieve any soreness in the muscles.

- Masking tape to keep casts and stints in place.

- Penicillin G for any infection.

- Betadine scrub.

- Hydrogen peroxide.

- A stethoscope.

- Sterile water.

Keep these necessary items in a box so that it can be used when necessary. Make sure that you replace bandages and the medicines every six months or as per the date of expiry.

6. Preventive care

Having some routine preventive care measures in place will help you ensure that you prevent any diseases from manifesting in the first place. This is the most effective way of making sure that your pig is safe and healthy.

- Make sure you follow the vaccination schedule given to your by your vet.

- Keep the hooves trimmed.

- Make sure that the housing area is well ventilated.

- Have ample clean water available for the pig at all times.

- Deworm your pig regularly to prevent internal parasites.

- Do not overcrowd the pigs in the housing area.

- If one of the pigs is infected, make sure that you isolate him immediately.

- Keep the skin clean and free from ticks and other parasites.

- Ensure that you follow a healthy diet plan for your pig.

- Keep the calorie intake in check to prevent issues related to being overweight.

- Provide adequate care during the warmer months to prevent heat strokes.

- Have enough resting areas available to the pig.

- Keep the housing area free from any drafts or cold winds.

These preventive measures will go a long way when it comes to the health of your pig. Make sure you have a check on these measures regularly to prevent any lapses.

7. Getting your Kunekune insured

When you get a Kunekune pig, it is best to have your pig insured. The expenses related to veterinary care can be quite high, as pigs are often classified as exotic animals.

When they fall seriously ill, you will have to shell out a lot of money to help them recover. One option is to put aside some money each month just for a medical emergency.

However, with Kunekune pigs, you have the advantage of pet insurance. There are several companies that offer insurance especially for pigs and other small mammals. Since their popularity as pets increased, several pet insurance companies are offering great insurance plans that keep your pig covered in case of serious illnesses.

Always check with your vet
Never buy any insurance without checking with your vet first. Some veterinary clinics are open to all types of insurance while others only work with certain veterinary companies. Make sure that you compare various policies before fixing on one to ensure that you can afford the premium each month.

There are several websites that allow you to compare various insurance companies. When you are choosing a pet insurance, make sure that it covers the following:

- Hospitalization
- X Rays
- Medical examinations
- Prescriptions.

Check for third party liability costs. This will also cover any damage caused by your pet to a third party.

Best insurance plans for pigs
Here is a list of some of the best insurance plans available for pet pigs:

Pet Assure

Pet Assure is considered one of the best companies when it comes to insurance for exotic animals. Here are some features of this plan:

- It has two options: a single plan and a family plan.

- With the single plan, you can get 25% off on all your medical services. In addition to that, you have a 50% discounts on any merchandise or pet products that you purchase.

- In case of any lost pig, you also get monitoring services until the pig is recovered.

- For a monthly single plan, you have a processing fee of $10 or £5 while the annual plan has no processing fee.

- The average yearly premium for a small pig like the Kunekune is $79-$99 or £30- £50 for a single plan.

- The family plan allows you to insure up to 4 pigs at one time.

- The premium for the family plan is about $140 or £75 annually.

VPI Pet Insurance

This is a plan that covers several diseases and offers great coverage. Here are some features of this plan:

- The pig can be insured against accidents, illnesses, chronic diseases, injuries and even some forms of cancer.

- There are two plan options with this insurance as well: VPI Standard and VPI Superior.

- In the case of any unrelated accident you have the option of $50 deductible in both the plans.

- VPI superior plan has a larger reimbursement of about $14,000 or £7500.

- The reimbursement with the VPI standard plan is $9000 or £4500.

Lester Kalmanson Agency Inc.

This plan gives you two great features:

- You have great coverage for rare diseases and the reimbursement depends on the breed; whether it is a rare or domestic pig.

- You also have insurance for a pig that is in transit in case of any international transportation.

If an insurance plan seems unaffordable to you, then you may want to reconsider brining a pet pig home. Make sure you have enough funds available before you commit to a pet pig.

Conclusion

A responsible pet parent is one who tries to learn as much about their pet as possible. This book is aimed at helping you do just that. It is a step by step guide to good pig husbandry.

Thank you for choosing this book to learn all about Kunekune pigs. The book is a result of extensive research and learning from Kunekune pig owners to bring you information that is authentic and practical. Hopefully, you are able to find all the queries that you may have about your pig from the moment you bring one home.

Remember to keep yourself updated about the health and well being of your pig along the way. This will help you understand about any medical advancements or better options to provide the best possible care for your beloved Kunekune pigs.

Kunekune pigs are wonderful companions and you can be sure that your journey with your pet will be nothing but joyful and fulfilling.

References

Note: at the time of printing, all the websites below were working. As the internet changes rapidly, some sites might no longer be live when you read this book. That is, of course, out of our control.

There are several online sources that help you learn more about Kunekune pigs. You can also participate in live discussions to learn more about your pet. Although Kunekune pigs are getting more popular by the day, it is hard to find people who have enough experience with them. Here are some online platforms that bring together several experts and Kunekune owners to resolve this issue.

- www.minipiginfo.com
- www.petpigeducation.com
- www.healthypigs.easystorecreator.com
- www.prairiecreekkids.com
- www.britishkunekunesociety.org.uk
- www.specialbreeds.co.uk
- www.ecofarmingdaily.com
- www.pigs4ever.com
- www.animal-nutrition.wikia.com
- www.americankunekunepigsociety.com
- www.permies.com
- www.thepigsite.com
- www.daf.qld.gov.au
- www.grit.com
- www.pigpalssanctuary.com
- www.micropigpets.com
- www.regalpet.com
- www.bestfriends.org
- www.lifewithaminipig.com
- www.charmingminipigs.com
- www.squealsonwheels.us
- www.kewlittlepigs.com
- www.lilorphanhammies.org
- www.petpigs.com
- www.spca.bc.ca
- www.pigplacementnetwork.org
- www.americanminipigassociation.com

- www.forfarmers.co.uk
- www.pennywellfarm.co.uk
- www.theresearchpedia.com
- www.petassure.com
- www.msdvetmanual.com
- www.pig333.com
- www.pinoynegosyo.net
- www.farmersweekly.co.za
- www.avianexoticsvet.com
- www.americanminipigrescue.com
- www.pawstoclawsvetcare.com
- www.coloradocutiepigs.com
- www.gov.uk
- www.businesscompanion.info
- www.lovelivegrow.com
- www.pets.costhelper.com
- www.animals.mom.me
- www.farmersweekly.co.za
- www.nzdl.org
- www.redroofkunekune.com
- www.theteenytinyfarm.com
- www.woburnsafari.co.uk
- www.news.nationalgeographic.com
- www.iagfarm.com
- www.kunekune.co.nz

Made in the USA
Columbia, SC
21 March 2021